ERNIE GIFFORD was born in 1928 and, after an exciting boyhood through the war years, he progressed to manhood and married at quite an early age. He and his wife had five children, but unfortunately the marriage didn't last, and after twenty-three years Ernie left home.

Ernie met Margaret, they got married and have enjoyed their life together and particularly the fifteen years they were involved with American Football.

# MILTON KEYNES AMERICAN FOOTBALL CLUB

# THE PIONEERS

*Forgotten Champions*

# MILTON KEYNES AMERICAN FOOTBALL CLUB

# THE PIONEERS

*Forgotten Champions*

*Ernie Gifford*

ATHENA PRESS
LONDON

MILTON KEYNES AMERICAN FOOTBALL CLUB
*The Pioneers: Forgotten Champions*
Copyright © Ernie Gifford 2010


All Rights Reserved

No part of this book may be reproduced in any form
by photocopying or by any electronic or mechanical means,
including information storage or retrieval systems,
without permission in writing from both the copyright
owner and the publisher of this book.


ISBN 978 1 84748 739 1


First published 2010 by
ATHENA PRESS
Queen's House, 2 Holly Road
Twickenham TW1 4EG
United Kingdom


Printed for Athena Press

## *Cameo of the Author*

When I was asked to write a few words about Ernie Gifford, I struggled. Not because there is little to say about this larger-than-life character. Nor was it because I could think of only negative things. No, it was simply because no amount of written words can truly do justice to this remarkable man.

I first met Ernie in 1985. From the outset I knew that this man would have a profound influence on my life. Here was a man dedicated to his team, a man who was full of fun and life, and a man whose loyalty was unquestioning.

Throughout my long association with Ernie I have spent many enjoyable hours in his company. He has regaled me with his interesting experiences, his philosophy of life and shared his legendary humour.

Dedication is something that every true sportsman needs, and no one could be more dedicated to his team. A measure of this dedication can be demonstrated by a simple example. Every year each team had to register its players and receive identity cards in return. Each year teams struggled with late or missing cards. The Pioneers never had that problem. Ernie (accompanied usually by myself) would drive the long distance from Milton Keynes to Boston in Lincolnshire to the league offices, to ensure that the Pioneers' registrations were completely up to date and all players were eligible.

Ernie is a character. He is humorous, loyal, intelligent, dedicated and a thoroughly good bloke. His wit is dry but decisive. He can turn a negative into a positive with consummate ease.

To try and sum Ernie up in a few words on paper is impossible. Ernie has so many different layers and facets to his character that it is beyond me to do him justice.

It has been a privilege to know Ernie, and I thank the day that I met him. He has been a rock when I needed him, a sympathetic ear when the occasion called for one, but most of all I am proud that I can call him friend.

Brian Day

## *Forethought*

In the following pages I have endeavoured to illustrate the trials and tribulations of getting heavily involved in the running of a sports club.

As you will see, it does have its funny side, and it can also be very rewarding, besides being sometimes downright exciting.

The strangest thing about all this is that I have never been particularly interested in sport of any kind, but for some obscure reason this particular sport sparked an interest that I simply could not ignore, and I must admit that I have not regretted a single minute – although it has cost Margaret and me an awful lot of money, the details of which I have explained in the text of the book.

Having now retired completely from any managerial or other task connected with the sport, the only contact we have is that we do support the London Mets, as quite a few of our lads joined that team when the Pioneers finally broke up. Also Brian Smallworth, the Mets' general manager, has made Margaret and myself lifetime members, which is very gratifying, as it entitles us to a free meal at their home games.

Little did I know when I attended an American Football game, in which my stepson was taking part, that it would lead to a consuming passion – and almost an obsession – that would be a large part of my life for the next fifteen years. Those fifteen years have been a roller coaster of emotions, from the ecstasy of winning the Division 2 Championship in 1994, to the despair of that final dark season when the team folded after Margaret and I retired. I have covered the whole gamut of emotions from joy, happiness and laughter, to sadness, frustration and ultimately bitterness. If I could go back over those fifteen years, there are things I would have done differently, decisions I would not have made, arguments I would have avoided, and I might have enjoyed the happy times just a bit more than I did.

This book tells of my involvement with the two Milton Keynes teams, the Milton Keynes Bucks and the Milton Keynes Pioneers. It details the progress the teams made throughout the years, and reflects my passion for the sport of American Football.

I have tried to mention as many names and incidents as I can remember. Some of these memories may be flawed with the passing of time, and some names have just faded away in the distance. I hope that any omissions or inaccuracies do not spoil your enjoyment of the book.

I would like to thank those people who helped me with the compilation of this book, namely Brian Day for helping me fill in the facts and for finding relevant details that I was a bit hazy on; and I would also like to thank Bob Wade for his technical support on the computer.

Most of all I would like to thank my wife, Margaret. Margaret has put up with my obsession for American Football over the years, and even became involved herself, as you will discover in the following pages. She has been a tower of strength in aiding the running of the clubs, especially the Pioneers. Margaret was always there to act as counsellor and restraining influence when my ambition threatened to run away from the everyday realities of life. Finally she has put up with the hours I have spent huddled over the keyboard while compiling this book, and also spent hours proofreading for me.

I hope you enjoy this book and find it as interesting to read as I have found it to be in the writing.

They say that it is only a game, but American Football – especially in the city of Milton Keynes – has been more a way of life than a game!

Ernie Gifford

## *Forgotten Champions*

Hi, my name's Ernie Gifford. My wife, Margaret, and I would like to tell you all about our experiences helping to run an American Football Club here in England. I understand that the game was introduced to England in the winter of 1982 with Channel 4 Television showing matches live from the USA. Then in 1983 people in London were very surprised to see a bunch of lads running about in Hyde Park apparently trying to injure each other. This was the beginning of what turned out to be the birth of a new sport in this country, with the formation of teams, the first of which was the London Ravens, followed by a host of others, including Milton Keynes, Birmingham, Nottingham, Leicester and Manchester, to name but a few, until altogether there were about thirty-five teams all over the country.

Another event that helped to fuel interest in the game was when, in June 1983, the NFL sent over two teams to play in the first American Bowl at Wembley Stadium. The teams involved were the Vikings and the Cardinals, and the game was very well supported with a near capacity crowd who witnessed a resounding victory for the Vikings with a score of 28–10.

It was also in this year that the first domestic game of American Football was played in this country, the game being between the London Ravens against Northwich Spartans, who later became known as the Manchester Spartans. Milton Keynes was among the first cities to set up a team, and it was aptly named the Milton Keynes Bucks, which was very subtle, as when a resident wrote their address, the last line was Milton Keynes, Bucks.

One of the first games played by the Bucks was against the RAF Wyton Eagles, an all-American team. I never witnessed the game, but I am reliably informed that the result was a draw at 14–14, which was quite an achievement for a team of amateurs. The first game we went to watch was the Bucks against a team from Northampton called the 'Stormbringers'. The reason we went to the match was because my stepson, Robert, was playing and he asked us to go and watch. The match was one of a series of friendlies to be played at the Milton Keynes Bowl and attracted a crowd of around 4,000 people. The game also introduced the team's cheerleaders, the 'Buckeroos'.

*England v. France, 1984, played at Walton-on-Thames
Margaret holding 'Buckerwotsit'*

The weather was very hot and sunny and the crowd enjoyed sunbathing, barbecues and watching a very exciting game. If I remember rightly the score was 20–18 to the Bucks; it was a very close thing and the result was decided by a missed field goal in the dying seconds of the game. Needless to say, everybody had a great day, and I decided that I would carry on helping out where necessary, as the game had fired up my enthusiasm. Margaret also got involved with selling all sorts of things to help in fund-raising, and one thing she did do was to make a mascot of a weird animal she called a 'Buckerwotsit'. The amusing thing was that Radcliffe Philips, the founder of the Bucks, said that this mascot was now the property of the Bucks. I'm afraid I cannot repeat what Margaret told him to do with his ideas, and she would not be making any more anyway.

I decided to make a flag bearing the team's logo, which was a stag's head, and went to work by scrounging a white double sheet from Margaret. I then cut it into three panels and traced the logo onto two of the panels, then proceeded to paint the logo with the paint used for models, plus the appropriate wording. Then when they were dry I put them together with the blank panel in the middle so as you couldn't see through it. When I took the flag to a match it was accepted with delight, and as a result I was commissioned to make some more. I finally ended up making four. I also made a banner for the cheerleaders, the 'Buckeroos', and at the match that I presented them with it, it was stolen!

Now might be a good time to acquaint you with a basic idea of the make-up and rules of this game, as I have learnt them from reading and watching. The game is, as you have probably gathered, based on our game of rugby. Firstly, the team can register as many players as possible, although they are only allowed forty-five on the sideline at a game. The reason is that, unlike in soccer, they can substitute players for every play, if necessary, depending on the type of play that has been called. The number of players on the field at any time is eleven for each team, and having too many on the field, which sometimes happens, incurs a penalty. The team consists of three elements, offense, defense and special teams. Now, I think that the offense and defense are self-explanatory, so I will deal with special teams. This group of players are used for kick-off and punt situations and are nicknamed the 'Suicide Squad'. This is because, as the ball is kicked, they all dash hell for leather down the field to endeavour to make sure that the ball is not returned too far upfield, because the next play will start from wherever the ball is grounded.

Now the offense and defense take up their positions. The offense has four opportunities or *downs* to move the ball ten yards. They can do this by either running or passing the ball. In rugby they are allowed to pass backwards only as many times as they like, whereas in American Football, besides being able to pass laterally and backwards, they are also allowed *one* forward pass. If they succeed in moving the ball ten yards or more then the chains are moved and they get another four downs. (I'll explain about the chains later.) If they do not make the ten yards on third down, then on fourth down they have the option to attempt to make the necessary yardage, or punt the ball as far downfield as possible; and then, as with the kick-off, to limit the opposition to as little yardage as possible, they then change possession for the other team to have a go.

As promised, I will now explain the purpose of the chains. The chain crew consists of three members, two to hold the chains and one to hold the down marker. The chain is ten yards long, stretched between two poles to indicate the distance the offense has to move the ball in the four attempts or downs as explained earlier. There is a marker that is attached to the chain and this is situated where the chain coincides with one of the five- or ten-yard lines, and is moved each time the chains are repositioned by the person who is in charge of the down marker. The purpose of this is for when, if the ball is very close to making a first down, the officials have to measure. The down marker is also a pole with the numbers one to four at the top to show the spectators which down it is and is positioned where the next play is to start from and to indicate how far the offense have moved on each down.

Obviously the object of all this is to get the ball over the goal line for a *touchdown*, which is worth six points. It is worth noting that to score the touchdown the ball does not necessarily have to be grounded, as in rugby. This is followed by the *point after attempt*, which if kicked over the bar is worth one point; if passed or run over the line it's worth two points. Two other ways to score are firstly by a *field goal*, worth three points, or if you catch one of the opposition in the end zone in possession of the ball, or if the ball is snapped and goes over the head of the player and rolls out of the end zone, it's a safety, worth two points.

Now for the officials. For our games we usually have five, but on occasion that is reduced to four, depending on how many games are being played on any particular weekend, as the number of officials available is governed by how many men are on duty. But on important games, like finals and bowl games, it goes to seven. Now the teams have to pay the officials, and in the earlier days of the game we used to have to pay travelling expenses as well. As you can imagine, £30 per man plus expenses made this one of the most expensive aspects of the sport, especially as it seemed that they made up the crews with people who lived a long way away. I hope this gives you some idea of the workings of the game; of course, there are certain other refinements, i.e. penalties etc., which I won't go into at this point as I'm still learning myself.

Now to be honest I have never had much interest in sport, as I've mentioned before, but Margaret and I were very taken with this particular sport, and as you will see we got ourselves really and truly caught up in this new phenomenon. We did carry on and watched several more matches, and once we began to understand the rules we tended to enjoy them more and more. One of the problems that came to the fore was that the game, although basically sixty minutes long, tended to last on average three hours! This was because every time the ball went dead the clock stopped. Also each team had three ninety-second timeouts in each half to discuss strategy, plus they had an automatic timeout with the two-minute warning given before the end of each half – the only problem being that those two minutes could last an awful long time! This made things rather difficult keeping the interest of the spectators, hence the introduction of half-time entertainment, and the recruitment of cheerleaders. Furthermore, at the commencement of each play the referee blew his whistle, then the centre had twenty-five seconds to snap the ball.

I would now like to introduce something about the workings of the officials. These are very dedicated men whose sole purpose in life is to ensure that the game is played fair and above board. Their job can be very frustrating, and they have to be quick in assessing the validity of the play, and be seen to be giving the correct judgement on the outcome.

On p.17, I have included some of the most common hand signals as given by the referee. To indicate an infringement of the rules, the official closest to the misdemeanour throws a yellow flag onto the pitch. The officials then gather together to ascertain the degree of severity of the incident. When agreement is reached, the referee faces the supporters and delivers the punishment, which could vary from five to fifteen yards and could definitely affect the outcome of the game.

Also it should be borne in mind that a flag can be thrown, not only on players, but also on the misbehaviour of sideline personnel and even spectators, such as swearing at the officials. There is not a lot more I can say about this subject without going into an enormous amount of unnecessary detail, which in all truthfulness I might not get right, and really this is only to acquaint you with the basic rulings of the game in general.

## Most Common Official Signals

When something happens on the field that involves the officials, the referee communicates what has happened to the fans, and the television audience, via a microphone and a set of hand signals.

| | | | |
|---|---|---|---|
| Offside or encroaching |  Holding |  Illegal motion |  First down |
| 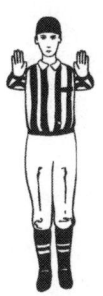 Pass interference |  Incomplete pass, penalty refused |  Illegal contact |  Delay of game |
|  Time out |  Touch down, field goal |  Personal foul |  Illegal use of hands |

## *1984*

This year saw the introduction of the first organised games and the formation of leagues. There was the BAFF (British American Football Federation) and the American Football League UK (AFL, UK). Radcliff Philips was appointed Financial Director of the AFL (UK) and meetings were held in the Amway building at Tongwell. I recall one meeting I went to, Radcliff was on the telephone and raised his hand for us to be quiet as he claimed that he was talking to the 49ers in America. Whether this was true or not, I have never been able to find out, although having said that the first game shirts used by the Bucks were donated by the 49ers, which gave rise to the club colour being burgundy. This resulted in the Bucks' defense being called the 'Burgundy Beasts', a nickname they earned through their aggressive approach to the game. Also two other leagues appeared on the scene namely the UKAFA (UK American Football Association) and the AAFC (Association of American Football Clubs).

Radcliff was very good at getting sponsorship, and I know for a fact that he managed to get £15,000 from Whitbreads. He also arranged a deal with Cowley and Wilson, a car dealer in Milton Keynes, which I'll tell you about later. There were other deals but I don't know the details.

As I stated earlier, I was getting myself involved and early in the year the Bucks took on a team from France, the Paris Blue Angels, and the founder of the Bucks, Radcliff Philips, approached me and asked if I would organise accommodation for the French team by putting them up with our team members. It took some time getting the team settled, but finally everyone was catered for, and Margaret and I agreed to take in the quarterback and his wife. He could speak a little English but his wife could not speak any, but in spite of this we got on very well, and on their first night with us we introduced them to home-made shepherd's pie, which was received with great relish.

The game was played at the Milton Keynes Bowl in atrocious weather conditions, and I believe (as I was rather busy organising the other activities to do with the game) that the Bucks lost, with a scoreline of 12–27 in France's favour. I do remember, however, struggling to erect a tent in a gale, in which we were selling all sorts of memorabilia, and we even had a bran tub for the kiddies, besides generally trying to get everything in order for the game. After this episode, Radcliff invited me round to his house and asked me if I would take on the running of the supporters' club, or Booster Club, as he called it. Not having had any previous experience of this sort of responsibility, I was a little hesitant, but I overcame my misgivings and decided to give it a go. To my surprise, and I must admit pleasure, club membership increased from forty-five to 120, which I feel vindicated my efforts.

Another game that was played during this year was an international between England and France. The match was played in Walton-on-Thames and I had to organise the coaches for the players and supporters. There were two coaches of supporters, so the England team were well represented from this region. The atmosphere at this game was tremendous, and after a very tense match England were the winners, with a scoreline of 7–0. After the game it became a bit of a wild party, with the supporters and the teams performing high jinks on the area adjacent to the stadium. The lads from the French team were going round begging for us to give them our T-shirts and caps as souvenirs. One lad tried to persuade my wife to part with her T-shirt, to which she replied, 'On your bike, son!' So I lost mine instead and had to go home shirtless, but as I said a great time was had by all. It was also at this game that the new publication, *First Down*, was introduced. This was a newspaper all about the game, here in England and also the USA, and was heralded with the handing out of free copies.

The Bucks were now on the road to Charlton's soccer ground to play the Greenwich Rams. This turned out to be a very entertaining match. In the stand behind us was a coloured lad with a voice that needed no microphone, as it resounded across the stadium. He was a Greenwich supporter, and every time his team got the ball his cry was 'Give the ball to Terry!'

This went on all throughout the game and caused some hilarity, but unfortunately the Rams were losing, and we said, 'Well, what about Terry now?' He just replied, 'He hasn't been very well lately.' A truly sporting supporter!

Another match that stands out in my mind was one we played at King's Lynn. The weather this time was the exact opposite of the last game, with thunder, lightning and torrential rain. I had hired a minibus and the field we played on was extremely muddy; needless to say I got the bus stuck in the mud, and at the end of the game I had to get the lads to push me out. The game itself was not without drama. Because of the persistent rain the cheerleaders were doing their chants dressed in dustbin liners, and one of the coaches, Mr Delaney, sat in the back of the minibus with tissues stuck up his nose, as he was suffering with an acute attack of sinusitis. In addition, one of the opposition's players, after a tackle, was under a pile of bodies with his face in a puddle and almost drowned – and what's more he also broke his leg in three places! We successfully managed to get him to the ambulance and on to the hospital. We also had to postpone the game for fifteen minutes because of lightning, and a couple who were on top of a scaffolding platform were almost struck. I can assure you that they came down from their perch quicker than they went up! I'm afraid that I cannot remember the score but I am under the impression that the Bucks won.

In May, the Bucks were invited to take part in a spectacular organised by the Waterways Board down by the Grand Union Canal, and the opponents were the Herts Phantoms. This was where I first met George Cunningham, who was commentating. The game was well received by the crowd and George proved to be an extremely good commentator. It was at this game that Radcliff Philips played at quarterback, wearing number 19 shirt – a number, incidentally, that we eventually banned, for reasons I'll explain later. He managed to score a touchdown and celebrated by doing a rain dance, and it actually started to rain! As you will see later on, George played a very important role in the future of the game.

## *1985*

In January, I was out delivering letters to supporters and the roads and pavements were very icy. I had climbed up three steps to deliver a letter and on my return I slipped and fell down those three steps and severely twisted my ankle. I managed to complete my round, but on arriving home my ankle was severely swollen, so I was driven off to the hospital, where, upon investigation, and an X-ray, it appeared that I had torn the tendons in my ankle, so I ended up with my leg in plaster – much to the concern of my fellow committee members. However, it was only for about three weeks and did not affect me carrying out my duties. As I stated earlier, the Bucks did very well with a sponsorship deal with Cowley and Wilson, a local car dealer, with them supplying a van beautifully embellished with the team name and logo. The reason behind the offer was to transport the teams' equipment to and from their games, and the firm even supplied a driver.

This year saw the first organised league games, with the Bucks playing in the AFL (UK) against teams like Birmingham Bulls, Nottingham Hoods, Northants Stormbringers, Walsall Titans, King's Lynn Patriots and Warwickshire Bears (later to be the Coventry Bears).

It was a great year for the Bucks with an outstanding record of ten wins and just two losses, the ones against the Bulls, to put the Bucks in the forefront of the game in Britain. All the Bucks home games were played at the Milton Keynes Bowl, which I attended with Margaret, as we were responsible for erecting the tent for the memorabilia and also organising the placement of the other facilities. At one game they tried to put on a bit of a spectacle, with the Red Devils parachute team dropping in with the game ball. Unfortunately the Red Devils were held up and the timing went completely haywire, making the kick-off twenty minutes late. At another of the games, a marching band from Birmingham was brought in to entertain the crowds. The band was very flamboyant with uniforms of bright orange. Their conductor looked very commanding in his white suit and gave a very animated performance. They performed just prior to the game and at half-time, to the obvious delight of the crowd. These small additions to the afternoon made the games very entertaining and the crowds loved every minute.

## *1986*

On 3 March, two more NFL teams came over to play at Wembley. This time it was the Chicago Bears v Dallas Cowboys, and to everyone's surprise there was an attendance of 82,699 people, which proved the attraction of the game. The result of the game was a win for the Bears with a scoreline of 17–6. Of course, our domestic game was no match for these professional giants but we were steadily improving.

The Bucks were playing extremely well and making a name for themselves nationally.

One game I recall was against the Portsmouth Warriors, which was played in Waterlooville. This time we took three coaches, one for the players and two for the supporters. Margaret was in charge of one coach and I took over the other. On the way down our driver missed the turning and we ended up in Portsmouth docks. After charging around the countryside, we finally arrived at the ground with not a lot of time to spare before kick-off. The weather was extremely hot and humid and one of our players went down with dehydration, and had to be carried off the field. Worse, one of our best players, Gladstone McKenzie, pulled a hamstring at a crucial moment, in the process of scoring a touchdown; but the match was a close thing with the Bucks taking it 7–5.

The journey home was also a lot of fun, as when we stopped at a services on the way back we discovered that we had a young engaged couple with us, and I was trying to persuade them to get married during a game, at half-time, but they would have none of it. In fact, when we mentioned marriage the lad visibly blanched, so we had to assume that their relationship was not quite ready for that sort of commitment... Also during this stop another of our supporters decided to give us a song. He was sitting on a wall and got so carried away that he slowly disappeared as he fell backwards off the wall. He only had one arm, which made it difficult for him to recover his composure, but he treated the whole incident as a huge joke.

In an effort to boost the image of the team and the sport, Radcliff decided to hire Middleton Hall in the city centre. The hall is large and we had to divide it in half so as to give access for the public to cross to John Lewis's. One half was given over to the team for demonstrations and plays that were very carefully staged plays because of the tremendous amount of glass. The other half was used to set up a tombola stall and various other things to try to attract the people. I came up with the idea of using a Polaroid camera to take pictures of young children with some of the players and charge £1 for the print. I approached the local camera shop and managed to get ten films on sale or return. The films cost £7 each and produced ten pictures, which gave us a profit of £3 on each film used, and we managed to use seven out of the ten films.

Things did not look too good, as changes had been taking place at management level but the players were being kept in the dark so to speak. The major event that happened was Radcliff Philips forming the Bucks into a limited liability company. By doing this he thought that he owned a team, whereas all he owned was a name, and this he was to find out to his cost in the not too distant future.

It was during this season that events took a turn for the worse as the coach company we were using said that they would not supply coaches for further away games, as they were still owed money from previous trips, and it was only after Margaret promised to guarantee the cost that they relented, and we managed to finish the season. This situation proved to be intolerable, and as you will see the team reacted in the only way they could.

Everything came to a head at the end of the season when the players decided that, for reasons of their own, they would walk away from the management and approached Margaret, myself, Trina Collins and Gail Pyne with a request to reform the team. We agreed to do our best and set about contacting people whom we thought would be willing to help.

The next thing we had to do was to arrange an inaugural

meeting of everybody concerned, this we set up on 4 October 1986. The meeting was very well attended by all of the players and other interested parties, and the first priority was to elect a committee. We asked for nominations from the floor and when the voting was complete we had a committee consisting of: Chairman – Bob Wilcox (an American who expressed an interest); Ernie Gifford, Vice Chairman; Trina Collins, Secretary; Margaret Gifford, Treasurer; Gladstone McKenzie Sr, PR; Gail Pyne, Team Manager; and Brian Day, Programme Editor. We decided that this would be a players' club, so in order to give the players an interest in the running of the club, and to make sure that what happened to the Bucks didn't happen to us, we decided to co-opt two players on to the committee. We also felt that the sport was too young to consider forming limited companies, as the league structure at that time was too fragmented and sufficient funds were not available; also, media attention was practically non-existent, except for the local press and later local radio.

Next came the question of a name for the team, and also colours for the shirts and pants (we couldn't use the name Bucks, as it was registered). Eventually we had seven suggestions: Phoenix, Firebirds, Zulus (needless to say this was suggested by one of our coloured players, causing some hilarity), Tornados, Hurricanes, Pioneers and Bucks (as in dollars). Voting was a bit chaotic, but we eventually narrowed it down to two names: Phoenix and Pioneers. After a final round of voting the winning name was the Pioneers, which won by just two votes. It was decided that the team colours would be red shirts and silver pants and silver helmets, with white shirts for away matches.

We now asked for suggestions for a team logo, and eventually we settled on a design of a player standing with his left arm raised holding a torn shirt, which cost us £50 to the person who was purported to have designed it. However, it transpired that it was taken from a poster of a team in Holland; still, we had adopted it so it stayed. Initially it caused a bit of a furore among the other teams, as they reckoned it was too aggressive, but we stuck to our decision and eventually it was accepted.

One of our supporters, who worked in a printing firm, took a copy of the logo, and in place of the shirt he imposed a picture of

Radcliff Philips's severed head. This bought a strong reaction from Radcliff and he threatened to sue us. Needless to say, things simmered down and he eventually saw the funny side of it. It was also decided to drop the number 19 shirt because of the association it had with Radcliff Philips. This may sound a bit petty, but at the time feelings were very high with regard to the way the players had been treated. The other thing that was suggested was for a team motto, several ideas were put up and eventually it was decided to adopt two. They were: 'Achievement through honesty and integrity' and 'Out of the ashes came forth something great'. We used these in all our programmes and we promoted them as much as possible.

As a point of interest, Trina Collins only held the position of secretary very temporarily, as due to commitments she was unable to fulfil her duties to her or our satisfaction. This left a void, which we needed to fill as soon as possible. As luck would have it our quarterback's father, Mr Dave Sparkes, attended one of our training sessions and foolishly asked if there was anything he could do to help. As you can imagine, we jumped at the chance of filling the position and asked him if he would accept the role of Secretary. He agreed and I must say he did a very good job for the time he was in office.

Incidentally, Trina returned a while later and became our statistician, a position at which she became very proficient working alongside Anita Howe. She also held other positions on the committee at various times, including Chairman and Secretary.

Margaret, in her position as Treasurer, approached the NatWest Bank with a view to open a business account for the club. All went well for quite some time until we became the victims of fraud.

Margaret had instructed the bank that nothing was to be sent through the post as we would collect everything ourselves. The next thing we knew was our account had been debited to the sum of £1,000! Margaret was livid and the fraud squad were called in. It transpired that the bank had sent two chequebooks through the post, which we did not receive, and two cheques had been cashed. Now the point is that we had stipulated that any cheque we presented had to have two signatures. The two fraudulent cheques only had one, which did not match either of the two examples. After a short time, the bank agreed to make restitution and the matter was dropped.

Another point of interest was when the Great Britain team played a game against Holland on 16 November in Hilversum. A coach was laid on and several of us went to watch, incidentally one of the British team players was Gladstone McKenzie, who later came to play for the Pioneers. The coach left on the Saturday evening and we travelled overnight and arrived at the ground at about lunchtime. The match was very exciting and Great Britain came out the winners by 24 to 5. After the game the coach took us into Amsterdam, where we had about three hours to see as much as we could. We looked around for a place to have a meal, and inadvertently ended up in the red-light district, much to our surprise, as that was the last thing we were thinking of, then followed the long journey home.

We finished the year with a Dinner Dance held in Northampton, commemorating the virtual demise of the Bucks with an award for each of the players who had been involved. It was a great success, and we vowed we would continue the practise over the coming years.

*November 1987*

## 1987

With the 'Pioneers' name finally in place, we contacted the league to register the team and staff. We were gobsmacked when we were told that we couldn't register, as we were a new team, despite the fact that we were the old Bucks bar two players. It emerged that Radcliff Philips, after the team walked away, took the two players who stayed with him to Coventry and boasted he had merged with the Bears, renaming them the Coventry Milton Keynes Bucks. This move roused a great deal of anger among the Bears supporters and they made sure that it only lasted for one season.

To try and keep the interest of players and staff we organised a trip to the Open University to watch the Super Bowl. I decided to arrange the Union Jack and the Stars and Stripes flags on the curtain at the end of the hall. I hung the Union Jack and prepared to pin up the Stars and Stripes when Bob Wilcox said in a raised voice, 'You can't stick pins into the American flag – it's desecration!' It showed me just how much the Americans treasure their flag. The rest of the evening went off very well and we resolved to do it again.

Our season didn't look too promising either, so to try and dull the disappointment the committee set to work to organise some friendly games, ending up with a tally of seven. At the time we were struggling to find a home ground, and played our first match at Woughton Campus, in virtually an open field, against a team called the Chingford Centurions. The game turned into a mud bath as the weather was rather inclement. The Pioneers won the game 6–0 with a decisive touchdown from an eighty-yard run by Danny McAnuff.

The second game we played at Wolverton Football Club, where we had to set up some rugby posts we managed to scrounge, something that had never been seen in the long history of the football club. Digging the holes for the posts turned out to be more difficult than we thought, as the ground was very stony, and we had to avail ourselves of the services of a groundsman who was working on site. Our opponents on the day were the Manchester Sabres.

It was at this game that I earned a standing ovation. It happened this way. The morning was beautifully sunny, and when we'd finished marking out the pitch it looked really good, with the lines fairly glinting in the sun. Then, to my dismay, half an hour before kick-off, the heavens opened and washed all the lines away, so I had to try and remark the pitch in a very short time, with the rain still falling... Manchester were late arriving due to traffic problems on the M6, which gave me a little more time to complete my task. The Manchester team had several of the old Leigh Razorbacks players, who had a lot of experience, so they weren't going to be a walkover. The game was very tense and it was a quarterback sack that led to Tony Jordan's first touchdown. The two points extra were added by Danny McAnuff: 8–0. It was Tony who again scored with a pass reception and he lived up to his nickname of 'Snake-hips' by twisting his way into the end zone making the final score 14–0.

It was now time to travel to Bristol to take on the Blackhawks in our third game of the season. Tony Jordan scored on the third play of the game when he ran the ball in from seven yards: 6–0. The Blackhawks' quarterback was sacked four times and the defense forced a two-point safety to give the pioneers an 8–0 lead at half-time. After the break, the Pioneers kept up the pressure and finally Danny McAnuff broke through to score the first of two touchdowns plus the two points both times to make the final score 24–0.

Unfortunately the Bristol Blackhawks failed to turn up for the return match, which was very disappointing for us.

When we travelled to Manchester we had a bit of trouble finding the ground, and imagine our surprise when we arrived to discover that the Sabres had no goalposts, so of course we were unable to kick for the extra point or go for field goals. We still elected to play the game, although it wouldn't have been recognised by the league, and it was Manchester who scored first with a quarterback sack in the end zone for a two-point safety. They then added a touchdown with no extra point to go 8–0 up. It wasn't until the third quarter that the Pioneers managed to level the scores with a touchdown by Danny McAnuff, who returned a Manchester punt for fifty-five yards; the two points were added and the match resulted in a draw: 8–8.

Back home, we were a little concerned another team had been formed within the city limits, namely the Bletchley Bees. We contacted their manager, Kevin Grumble, to try to negotiate a merger, as it was clear that the area could not sustain two teams. Also, during the season we had been swapping players to help each other out, so the players themselves were consulted. After several meetings it was decided to go ahead with the merger and it was agreed that we would retain the name of the Pioneers, and the final arrangements were in place before the last match of the season, which, as you will see, turned out to be crucial.

Once again the NFL sent another two teams, for what was becoming an annual event, to play at the Wembley Arena. The match this time was Broncos v Rams and the attendance was down from the previous year at 72,786. The scoreline this time was 27 Broncos, 28 Rams.

We now had to travel to Barnsley for a match that turned out to be quite remarkable. I had hired a minibus for the trip and on the way we called into a service area for petrol, and on the way out I tried to chat up two girls to accompany us, but to no avail. When we arrived we had no idea that it was to be only the second game they had played, and as you will see we were to create a record. Eight of our cheerleaders, who we had decided were to be given the name of the 'Trailblazers' (to reflect the name of the team), had travelled with us and looked resplendent in their uniforms and certainly gave a good account of themselves.

The game began with the Pioneers dominating the play, with Des Williams, returning to the club from the Nottingham Hoods, starting the ball rolling with an early touchdown and Danny McAnuff added three more including a fifty-yard punt return, plus further scores from Junior McKenzie and Mark Radcliffe making it 46–0 at the end of the quarter. Even the defense got in on the act in the second quarter with a two-point safety. Danny got two more touchdowns, and Dion Peddle added another touchdown to make it 68–0 at the half. The Bears insisted on playing the second half and Danny started by returning the kick-off seventy-eight yards to score, then another punt return, this time for eighteen yards. And by the final whistle the Pioneers had taken the score to a record 128–0. However, the point of this story has nothing to do with the score but with the sportsmanship shown by their players both on the field and in the bar afterwards, as they said, and I quote: 'You beat us, so what! We learnt a lot about the game today.' There's no answer to that.

Milton Keynes Pioneers, although not yet in a league, faced their toughest challenge yet against Budweiser Premier side, Heathrow Jets. The Pioneers were slow to start and soon found themselves trailing by a Jets field goal. This fired them up but they were unable to prevent a Jets touchdown and found themselves 0–10 down at the change of ends. Early in the second quarter the Pioneers were back in the game, with Des Williams bulldozing his way over the line from five yards to score, but with no extra point, making it 6–10 at the half.

In the third quarter, the heavens opened, and the pitch being Astroturf, it soon resembled a lake, as the water lay in great puddles. We were standing on the sidelines getting extremely wet, but four of our lovely cheerleaders stayed on the sideline with us, egging the team on and getting themselves soaked to the skin, as they had only their skimpy uniforms on. At the end of the game as the girls walked across the pitch they got a standing ovation from the spectators in the stand, including the *Aces'* cheerleaders, who had sheltered there throughout the game. As a point of interest we discovered that some of the Jets players were playing in motorcycle helmets, as the cost of proper helmets was almost prohibitive, something which incidentally did not change over the years. The problem was that all American Football equipment had to be imported from the States, so what with import duties and the dealer's mark-up, the costs were not too surprising.

We also publicised the fact that the team was prepared to give demonstrations of their playing skills to the public who were, in the main, ignorant of the rules of this particular sport. As luck would have it, one of our players, who lived in Towcester, got us an invitation to open the school fête at Sponne School in

Towcester. The plan was that we opened the fête at two o'clock with a half hour demonstration, then after a break of half an hour, we would go out and do it again for the benefit of people arriving late. However, when the lads went out the second time they completely took over the fête. What they did was to remove their pads, shirts and helmets and put them on the children. They then set up mock plays involving the children, and the results were hilarious. One particular incident I remember was when the lads lined up with the team as the offense and the children, after a bit of intensive coaching, as the defense. As the ball was snapped, the boy who was opposite the centre dived straight between his legs and sacked the quarterback, much to his surprise.

This sort of situation continued throughout the afternoon, with the team also including the parents and teachers. It was not only the players who were involved, as the three cheerleaders who turned up proceeded to show the young girls some of the dance routines and practised some of the chants. Near the finishing time, I was talking to the headmaster and asked for his comments on the afternoon's activities. He remarked, 'It's been brilliant, we've not seen anything like it before.' And as a point of interest we were invited back the following year.

After this demonstration we were in great demand from various schools and clubs. Some of them asked how much we charged, and I said that we didn't stipulate a fee, but if they would like to make a donation to the club it would be very acceptable. One occasion comes to mind, when we were asked to give a show at an infants' school. As you can imagine the children were only knee-high to grasshoppers, but the lads insisted on dressing them in their pads and shirts. They did this to one little lad, and when they put on the pads you could just see his hands sticking out each side. Then they put on a helmet and the poor lad just toppled forward with his head resting on the ground! The lad's uncle was standing next to me and I swear he almost wet himself with laughter. These were great times and made everything worthwhile.

Referring back to the Bees: during their season they had played several games against teams such as the Redditch Arrows, Rugby Rollers, Tamworth Trojans and Stourbridge Pumas. Of these games they lost to the Arrows, but won against the Trojans, Rollers and Pumas.

As already stated, the merger came in time for the final game of the season against a first division team, the Cambridge County Cats; it was played at our new ground at Manor Fields, Fenny Stratford, where we had managed to collect the original goalposts used by the Bucks the previous year.

Playing against National League opposition, the Pioneers were not overawed by the occasion. The Pioneers' offense started brightly making seventy yards on their first drive, only to be stopped on the Cambridge three-yard line. The Cats replied with a devastating ninety-seven-yard run to open the scoring plus the extra point: 0–7. The Pioneers swept back immediately to score from a six-yard pass, no extra point: 6–7. The Pioneers continued their dominance with a fifty-one-yard run: 12–7. In the second period, they scored again from a three-yard run to make the half-time score 18–7.

After the break, the Pioneers continued their domination scoring six more touchdowns, three in each quarter. Danny McAnuff scored two, Allan Brown two, Tony Jordan one and Dave Galbraith one. As a point of interest, Allan Brown's second TD was a scintillating, impudent seventy-two-yard run, deceiving the opposition following a fake punt attempt, this on a fourth down and in theory too many yards to run, which made the final score 56–7. So, with a record of five wins, one loss and one draw we re-applied to join a league.

With reference to the goalposts that were used by the Bucks, we had managed to acquire them from the Development Corporation, courtesy of Mr Dave Hildreth a councillor, so it meant that we had to approach the football club and ask for permission to dig holes on the field to take the bases. The permission was duly granted, so we set to work and positioned the bases just outside their goal line. The bases were made up with a square steel plate to which was welded a square tube three feet long. On top of this was another plate with six bolts welded, three down opposing sides. On this plate was yet another plate, this time with a block welded in the middle to take the base of the goalpost itself. This block had two holes drilled through it to take the base of the post, so to erect them took two large bolts. So by inserting one bolt we could swivel the post to the upright position. Joined to this was a crossbar in two halves bolted to the upright; then on the ends of the crossbar were two long uprights forming the goal area. Finally, to erect the posts we had to first, assemble them then use a Land Rover to tow them into position.

## *1988*

My birthday was on 23 January, and this year I would be sixty. As it happened we had arranged a disco for the team, which luckily was set for my birthday. My youngest son and daughter turned up and contributed to a birthday party I will remember for always. They even produced a birthday cake decorated with sixty candles. The trouble was that the candle wax melted into the icing, but who cares? It's not many people have a birthday party with over 200 guests!

For the Super Bowl this year we arranged to congregate at the Super Bowl Bar in the Winter Gardens in Central Milton Keynes. The attendance was good, and we had T-shirts and sweatshirts on display in the bar, and everyone had a good time in very congenial surroundings.

Having proved our potential, the team was accepted into the Budweiser Premier Division, East Midlands Conference. As the number of teams had increased dramatically in the short time the game had been in existence, it was necessary to divide the country into conferences, to try and cut down on the amount of travelling required for teams to fulfil their playing commitments. Another point that came up was the inclusion of Americans. Initially there was a rule in place that a team could have no more that four Americans in the squad. Later the rule was changed to only two, one on offense and one on defense, but teams were not allowed to play them both at the same time, as obviously they would be proficient on either side of the ball. Now this rule upset a lot of teams, as most could not afford to import them, and teams in the south-east were able to call on players from the American bases in the area. The league also laid down rules for the import of players from the States, as I have explained later.

It was now that the behind the scenes work intensified, like having to register all the players and staff, and insist on everybody supplying passport photographs to attach to the application forms.

Also we had to set the level of subs and arrange for ambulance cover at all home games. Game days were going to be demanding of time and energy and started at around 8 a.m. firstly, we had to mark out the pitch, which I had done before, but it was still a daunting task as the number of lines required were legion. Initially there were the side and end lines, then there was a line across the pitch every five yards except for the ten-yard end zone, there followed short lines (two feet long) every yard down each sideline. These were known as 'hash marks' and there were another two lines of 'hash marks', down the centre of the pitch eighteen feet apart. Then there were numbers on the ten-yard lines i.e. G 10 20 30 40 50 40 30 20 10 G. These had to be twenty-seven feet in from the sideline and were supposed to be six feet high, ours were three feet. Plus there was also the players' box, which was between the twenty-five-yard lines and marked six feet deep. This job usually took four people about three to four hours to complete, however over the seasons we managed to cut the time down significantly. Besides the pitch marking there were other jobs to be done, such as sorting out the shirts and pants for the players, setting up the table for the Gatorade, organising the chain crew and ball boys and making sure everything was in place for the officials. Then we needed someone on hand to welcome the visiting team and conduct them to the changing rooms.

Margaret and I used to make our own wine at this time, and we had the idea to raffle some on our journeys to away games. With this in mind we approached the police to ensure that we weren't breaking the law, and were pleased when they told us that as long as we didn't try to sell it, and only raffled it within the clubs membership, we were in the clear. So, as you can imagine, some of our journeys became very interesting, to say the least. The other thing we introduced was a 'sweetie jar' for the supporters and later for players. Incidentally, this became synonymous with the name of the Pioneers.

Our first Head Coach was Marc Walker, an American who was initially with the referees, and was based at Upper Heyford Air Base. He was highly respected by the players and demanded perfection from both the players and himself. Before the season proper we took on the Chiltern Cheetahs in a friendly match at

Fenny Stratford. The Pioneers failed to make any impact in the opening minutes of the game, and it was the defense that took over and produced the first score. The Cheetahs' quarterback was chased into his own end zone, and Conroy Brown promptly sacked him for a two-point safety. There was no further score in the first half, but when the Pioneers came out for the second half they had switched quarterbacks. Simon Sparkes was rested and Butch Peddle took over; he managed to connect with Mark Ratcliffe with a pass into the end zone to increase the score to 8–0. In the fourth quarter, Butch Peddle again launched a long pass to where Mark Benson completed the catch in the end zone for a further six points: 14–0. The final scoring move of the battle came when Simon Sparkes, back on the pitch, connected with Mark Benson to make the final score 20–0: a very good result and one we hoped to improve on. Following the final whistle, and after the players from both teams had crossed the pitch giving high fives, people were surprised to see the Pioneers form a circle and, holding hands, go down on one knee as Marc Walker led them in a short prayer. This rather pleasant ritual was repeated after every game while Marc Walker was in charge.

Our next friendly preseason game was away to the Walsall Titans, and the result showed how much we needed to train before the start of the season proper. It was Walsall who opened the scoring with a touchdown plus the two points after: 0–8. The Pioneers' reply was decisive, with Simon Sparkes connecting with Danny McAnuff for the score 6–8. Then following an interception, Danny McAnuff set up Eif Williams for the touchdown and Ray Davies added the extra point 13–8. Conroy Brown then added a second two-point safety to bring the score at the end of the first quarter to 15–8. The second quarter began with Butch Peddle handing off to Danny Carnegie for a ten-yard touchdown but no point after: 21–8. After a Pioneers fumble, the Titans completed a ten-yard pass making it 21–14; then once again the Pioneers took over and scored another touchdown and added the extra point to bring the half-time score to 28–14.

With the game seemingly won, the Pioneers then proceeded to throw it away, as the fourth quarter belonged almost exclusively to the Titans. Firstly an interception of a Matt Eden pass set the

Titans up to close the gap, and then uncharacteristically sloppy play allowed the home side to draw level at 28–28. Our last preseason game was against the Witney Wildcats to be played at our home ground at Manor Fields, and we were hoping to show an improvement on our previous game. The Pioneers opened the scoring with an early touchdown and it was a much more positive display as they limited the Wildcats to the minimum of possessions: 6–0. The second quarter was again evenly matched with both teams working hard to make the break through. On a fourth down play the Pioneers sent on the field unit and Ray Davies slotted the ball between the uprights to make the score 9–0 at half-time.

The third quarter was scoreless as both teams struggled to make a breakthrough; then in the final period the Pioneers thought they had scored only to have it called back for a penalty. From then on it became a hectic battle, but to no avail, with the score remaining at 9–0.

It was at one of our training sessions that one of our players, George Janeki, approached us and said that he had a surprise for us. He disappeared outside and reappeared carrying a large box followed by further boxes. Upon investigation it transpired that contained in the boxes was a brand new word processor, including a printer, which George said we could hold free for one year. As you can imagine, we were absolutely gobsmacked and extremely pleased. It meant that we could now do away with the aged typewriter that we had been using and write, print and store all of our paperwork on disk. The first thing that I did was to contact the managing director of the company which supplied the equipment and ask about what we should do if we needed servicing, etc.; he just said to contact him and the company would deal with it, and they even supplied the disks and printer ribbons!

Our fixture list included teams like Rockingham Rebels, West Bromwich Fireballs, Cambridge County Cats, Coventry Bears, and King's Lynn Patriots.

To open the season, we went off to Kettering to take on the Rockingham Rebels in the first of our league games. The Rebels fumbled the ball on their first possession, and Tom Cregg recovered it. After two long catch completions, the Pioneers reached the one-yard line from where Eric Stone caught the ball in the end zone, and Ray Davies, with the kick, made it 7–0. In the second quarter, the Rebels split the defense wide open and made the touchdown but failed to convert, to make the score 7–6. A Rebels punt was returned by A D Graham and gave Danny McAnuff the opportunity to run in for the score. Then Ray Davies again added the extra point to make it 14–6 at half-time.

After the break, both teams fought hard and furiously but there were no further scores, so the final result was 14–6. A good opening match for the Pioneers.

It was now time to meet the Cambridge County Cats for our second league game of the season at Manor Fields. There was no score in the first quarter as each side were evenly matched, and it wasn't until the second quarter that Butch Peddle broke the deadlock with an eight-yard pass to Eric Stone to put six points on the board. The Cats did not take long to reply after driving the Pioneers down to their own five-yard line from where their quarterback launched a five-yard pass to even the scores at 6–6, where they remained until half-time.

The third quarter seemed to last for an eternity as it was littered with penalties. The ball went back and fourth before Danny McAnuff put the Pioneers back in front when he caught a forty-one-yard pass from Butch Peddle: 12–6. Early in the final period, the Pioneers increased their score to 18–6 when Dave Chilman hauled in another Butch Peddle bomb, but the Cats came back immediately by returning the kick-off seventy-five yards to raise the score to 18–12. This seemed to sting the Pioneers into action, as Eif Williams ran twelve yards for the touchdown and Ray Davies kicked the extra point 25–12. The Pioneers then ran riot as Tim Blake rushed twenty-five yards then continued with a further ten yards to score, and Ray Davies again added the point after making the final score 32–12.

After travelling to Coventry, the crowd were kept on their toes with this Budweiser league clash of the Pioneers against Coventry Bears. The Bears fumbled on their first possession but the Pioneers were unable to capitalise on the mistake; but it was the Pioneers' defense that broke the deadlock when they sacked the Bears' quarterback in the end zone for a safety: 2–0. The Bears hit back straight away when they broke through the line for a touchdown: 2–6. It was only some great defensive work that prevented Coventry increasing their lead before the interval.

The Pioneers looked a different side after the break when Tom Cregg emerged from a melee to run eighty yards for a touchdown, 8–6, only for the Bears to hit back with a touchdown and point after to make it 8–13. It was then that our kicker, Ray Davies, scored a twenty-nine-yard field goal to bring the Pioneers within two points at 11–13. In the final period, the Pioneers backed the Bears down to their own one-yard line, from where Laurie Wallace and Pete Guerin added two points with a safety to make the game a very hard fought draw.

The Pioneers continued their unbeaten run with a home game against the West Bromwich Fireballs. The Pioneers forced a fumble on the first play and Simon Sparkes made a twenty-nine-yard pass to Danny McAnuff, which incurred a penalty for pass interference that put the Pioneers on the Fireballs' two-yard line from where Danny Carnegie bulldozed in for the score: 6–0. It was Simon Sparkes who again unleashed a twenty-five-yard bomb to connect with Dave Chilman pushing the score to 12–0. The Fireballs hit back with touchdown pass and went for the two-point conversion but were foiled, making it 12–6 at the end of the first quarter. In the second quarter, it was the Pioneers who dictated the game, with Simon Sparkes throwing a twenty-seven-yard pass to Leo Conoly, and at the end of the second quarter it was 18–6.

After the break, it was a case of jitters, as the Pioneers lost their momentum. They were backed up to their own end zone and conceded a safety when the snap went out of the end zone. The third quarter saw a lot of tough play and ended with a scoreline of 18–8. In the fourth quarter, the Fireballs closed the gap even further when they scored their second touchdown to make it 18–14. The tension mounted, and with just twelve seconds left in the game the Fireballs' quarterback launched a 'Hail Mary' pass, but it fell incomplete to give the Pioneers the win.

The Pioneers tightened their grip at the top of the Budweiser Premier League East Midlands Conference with a game against the King's Lynn Patriots in Norfolk. The weather was terrible with torrential rain, which saw Margaret walking around wearing a bin liner. Once more the first quarter was scoreless, then in the second quarter Danny McAnuff started things off with a fine jinking run for thirty-four yards to score, and Simon Sparkes kicked the extra point: 7–0. Danny McAnuff then dashed another twenty-six yards to score again, with Simon Sparkes again adding the extra point making it 14–0 at the half.

King's Lynn finally got on the scoresheet in the fourth quarter when the quarterback handed off to the running back and he made the end zone. The two-point attempt failed, leaving the score at 14–6. It was then that Danny McAnuff sealed a fine personal performance with a sixty-nine-yard sprint for the final touchdown to make it 20–6.

It was now time for the return match against the Rockingham Rebels at our home ground at Fenny Stratford. With Butch Peddle at quarterback, the Pioneers started well. They drove to the three-yard line, from where Junior McKenzie dived over the line to make the score 6–0 and Simon Sparkes kicked the extra point to make it 7–0. The rest of the first quarter was very even, with both teams playing hard but not being able to score. The second quarter saw Butch Peddle launch a long pass, which appeared to be heading as an incompletion, but Dave Chilman managed to haul it in for the touchdown: 13–0.

The second half was very unimpressive. The Pioneers, playing their second string players, struggled, and neither side looked likely to score. However, in the fourth quarter the Pioneers marched to the one-yard line after an impressive catch from Danny McAnuff. After being blocked twice by the Rebels, Eif Williams finally barrelled in to make the score 19–0. The point after attempt went wide of the posts, leaving the final score at 19–0.

The Pioneers suffered their first defeat of the season at Ely when the Cambridge County Cats proved that they were the team to watch. Cambridge dominated the first half, as in a near gale force wind they soon knocked up the points. Both Pioneers' offense and defense struggled as the Cats continued to pile on the points, and by the end of the first half they had scored thirty-two unanswered points.

In the third quarter, the Pioneers at last showed the form that had taken them so far in the season. Danny McAnuff and A D Graham worked exceptionally hard, and it was A D Graham who finally put some points on the board: 6–32. Disaster followed as Simon Sparkes was sacked and the ball landed in the hands of a defender who ran it in to push the score to 6–38. In the fourth quarter, Cambridge once again put together an impressive drive to enable their player to dive over the line for the touchdown; they also added the extra two points: 6–46. With little time left, Matt Eden hit Bob Miller with a ten-yard pass in the end zone; the two-point attempt was unsuccessful. With even less time remaining Cambridge completed the rout with another touchdown and the extra two points, bringing the final score to a humiliating 12–54.

In the next game against the Coventry Bears, the Pioneers got back to their winning ways, but it was a hard fought game. The Pioneers started brightly with some fine work from the running of Tony Jordan, returning to the team after a spell at the Nottingham Hoods. Butch Peddle starting at quarterback unleashed a fifty-two-yard pass to Danny McAnuff for the first score of the game: 6–0. The Bears replied with a thirteen-yard field goal making it 6–3. In the second quarter, the Bears fought back with a sixty-one-yard touchdown run, and the point after was good to make the score 6–10 in their favour at the end of the half.

The third quarter saw tough defensive play on both sides, as the Pioneers were determined to keep the scoring to a minimum, and the quarter was not a very inspiring one. If the third quarter was uninspiring the fourth quarter was electrifying, with A D Graham and Tony Jordan making a dynamic running attack, and the Pioneers started to dominate. Tony Jordan danced twenty-nine yards downfield before going over the line from six yards to score: 12–10. There was more excitement when A D Graham dashed twenty-three yards and dived full stretch over the goal line, but the officials adjudged that he had stepped out of bounds. With time running out the Pioneers played out the clock for a crucial win: 12–10.

With King's Lynn Patriots withdrawing from their league commitments we were awarded the game 1–0 by default.

However, we managed to arrange an inter-league match against the top BGFL team, St Albans Kestrels, which was played in a torrential downpour. The Kestrels opened the scoring when a punt snap went high over the head of the kicker and rolled out of the end zone for a two-point safety. In the second quarter, the Pioneers opened their account when Laurie Wallace crashed his way into the end zone, but no point after: 6–2. Disaster followed when a punt return was fumbled and recovered by St Albans. From the one-yard line they scored the touchdown again with no point after. Making the score 6–8 at half-time.

The third quarter saw the Pioneers step up a gear as twice they drove deep into Kestrels territory, and each time Tony Jordan found the end zone – firstly on a one-yard run, then ghosting his way in from the five-yard line, alas no points after: 18–8. The Pioneers wrapped the game up in the fourth quarter with one of the plays of the season. The handoff went to Danny McAnuff, he blasted his way downfield through a flock of Kestrels (please excuse the pun, I just couldn't resist it), and despite being chased by two Kestrels he found the end zone with an eighty-eight-yard run, making the final score 24–8.

An interesting development was that one of our American players, Chris (Bear) Groves, had his mother and sister, who unfortunately had a leg in plaster, visiting England, and they graciously came to watch the game. Now Mrs Groves was the spitting image of Elizabeth Taylor, which caused a few raised eyebrows. Anyway, she agreed to present an award to the winning team, the Pioneers, for which we were very grateful. The trophy was paid for and presented by Brian Day to mark this as a challenge match between our two leagues.

We now faced the West Bromwich Fireballs in the last of the regular season's games. We were flying high with only one defeat and one draw, and if we won this game the result between Coventry and Cambridge would decide whether or not we would win the Conference.

In the first quarter, the Pioneers snapped the ball for a punt. Unfortunately it sailed over the kickers head into the end zone, and on trying to retrieve it he was tackled for a two-point safety. After some very good defensive work, there was no further score in the period. After the change of ends, the Pioneers took control of the game, and following some good runs Butch Peddle passed to Eric Stone for a two-yard touchdown but no point after 6–2. Later in the quarter Tony Jordan rushed seven yards and Simon Sparkes added the point after, making it 13–2.

In the third quarter, after some more excellent defensive work Tony Jordan was able to rush three yards for his second touchdown, and the point after was added. With the start of the fourth quarter the heavens opened and there was no further scoring, leaving the final tally at 20–2.

We were on our way home after the match, and on the way Dave Sparkes telephoned the league. He came back to the coach with a huge grin on his face and announced, 'Congratulations, lads, you have become Conference Champions!' This meant that with our season's record we had home field advantage throughout the play-offs.

Now came our biggest test of the season – the play-off game against the Bristol Packers to be played at Manor Fields. The first quarter was a battle of the defenses as both sides fought to gain superiority in driving rain. Both teams showed the solid defense that had earned them a play-off position, so it was no surprise that the first quarter remained scoreless. In the second quarter, it was the Packers who opened the scoring with a rushing touchdown and a kicked point after: 0–7. With the Pioneers still reeling, they did it again, this time without the extra point, to make it 0–13 at the half.

The third quarter saw the Pioneers totally dominate without scoring, as despite an impressive drive they were unable to make that final push. Their only reward was a safety when Victor Brown tackled a Packer player after a fumble in the end zone: 2–13. The fourth quarter saw more dominance by the Pioneers but that touchdown still eluded them. The only highlight was a thirty-nine-yard reception by Danny McAnuff, which unfortunately he couldn't turn into a score, and the final score of 2–13 did not reflect the domination displayed by the Pioneers.

We had lost the play-off game but we were still Conference Champions, and we travelled up to Birmingham to the Bowl game to collect our trophy. We took quite a few of our supporters with us and they proved to everybody present that they could make more noise than anyone else when it came to supporting the team. Eif Williams and I went to collect the trophy, which was a beautiful cast model of an Eagle with its wings outstretched, and mounted on a wooden plinth. The shout that went up as we accepted it was tremendous and made everything worthwhile.

The annual NFL game, named the American Bowl, at the Wembley arena this year was between two of the best known teams, namely the Miami Dolphins and the San Francisco 49ers. Again the attendance was down slightly at 70,535. The result was a win for the Dolphins: 27–21. The popularity of these high level games was helping to boost the popularity of the domestic game, and it was a pity that the management structure was so fragmented, making it difficult to obtain sponsorship or credibility with the media.

Another milestone in our short history was an invitation to participate in the first ever Mayor's Parade. We decorated a float, which was particularly uninspiring, but with the lads and lasses (our cheerleaders, the Trailblazers) on parade, they were second to none. Dressed in their full game day uniform they looked rather intimidating, and the girls looked beguiling in their uniforms, so we gave them all collecting boxes and told them to go and collect. This they did with great gusto, hijacking buses and refusing to let them proceed until everyone had made a donation. This went on for some time until the police told them to stop, but people took it all in good part and I received a letter from the organisers (which was very tongue-in-cheek) thanking us for our efforts, as we had raised more money than anyone else.

Looking back to the spring, a section of the team was invited to participate on television in a programme on BBC2 called *Bazaar*, to give their opinions on home-brewed beer. The programme was produced at the BBC studios at the Open University, and lads really enjoyed making the programme, not only for the TV coverage, but also the chance to sample some free beer.

It was also during this year that we challenged an American team to a match; the team concerned was the Fighting Chicks, the team from Chicksands Air Force Base. The game was played on our home ground at Manor Fields, and despite all predictions of annihilation we held them to one touchdown and also denied them the extra point: 6–0. With this game we also got a limited amount of coverage on BBC East, and the team gave a performance which was a credit to all the members of the club.

On 16 October, Margaret and I went to a game which was played at Crystal Palace between two American college teams, namely Boston University and the University of Richmond. It so happened that Boston University jackets were the same colour as ours, so we chummed up with a chap who said he was the brother of Boston's quarterback. This didn't cut much ice until Simon Sparkes, our own quarterback, came and sat in front of us. As the game progressed Simon began to regret sitting where he did because every time the lad on the pitch made a good move, his brother gave Simon a hefty nudge with the comment, 'How about that, then!' Still, however good our friend thought his brother was, Boston were beaten in a very close game with a scoreline of Boston 17, Richmond 20.

Following our success at the Mayor's Parade we were invited to take part in the celebrations of the switching on of the Christmas lights at Woburn Sands, and at a briefing meeting before the event I met a lady from the St John Ambulance who said, 'I remember you from the Mayor's Parade, and I hope your lads will behave themselves as well as they did then.' The guest of honour for the town was Ted Rogers of TV fame.

We arrived at about two o'clock and the lads proceeded to do their callisthenics in the middle of the road, once again holding up traffic and waving collection boxes, but this time they were not quite so aggressive. The parade then followed with Ted Rogers riding on the top of an open topped bus and the lads marching along behind. The participants in the parade assembled in the yard of Plysu's factory on the outskirts of the town, then proceeded to march into town. On arrival in the town centre the lads decided to kidnap Ted and hold him to ransom; unfortunately, nobody was interested in saving him, so we had to let him go. However, we did manage to sign Ted up as an honorary member of the supporters' club. The cheerleaders also put on a good show, which attracted the crowds, and the lads then took over the stand of the local radio. Still, it was great fun and helped to get us known around the area.

We managed to secure some sponsorship from various companies, much of which was thanks to the sterling efforts of one of our players, Tom Cregg, who was an employee of Mercedes Benz, and he stayed with us throughout our involvement with the team. The council also introduced a scheme which matched any new sponsor's donation pound for pound to a maximum of £4,000. This was very useful in our endeavours to keep the club alive. To give you some idea of the running costs, it averaged out to around £10,000 to £15,000 per annum, and raising that sort of money did present a few problems. The costs included hire of the ground, payment to game day officials (there were up to six per game, as previously mentioned), an ambulance, which was mandatory, hire of coaches for away games, etc.; Then there were sundries, i.e. strapping tape, various medicines, tablets and lotions for burns and bruising, and of course spares for the equipment. Regarding that last item, one of our players managed to obtain a box full of spares for the helmets, which came to be very useful, and also incidentals such as printing, etc. We also had to pay for the services of a physio and some of the coaches, among others.

Margaret proved beyond any shadow of doubt to be the person to handle the financial affairs of the club, and she won the respect of everybody. Margaret's success was due to her experience of bookkeeping, and the fact that she insisted on issuing a receipt for every penny received (much to the annoyance of some players). Her methods paid off as at the end of the financial year she produced a statement accounting for every penny received and spent. The Pioneers proved to be one of the few clubs in the country to remain viable throughout their existence. It might be of interest to note that during her time with the club, Margaret took out two personal loans of £1,000 each to ensure that the club remained afloat.

At the end of the season we held a Dinner Dance, as promised, for all the players and their partners, and including members of staff and other interested parties. We had to make a nominal charge to cover costs but this was accepted without question. The venue we decided on was the Woughton House Hotel, which was in quite a secluded position and was very reasonable. The evening began with a three-course meal. Then the rest of the evening was taken up with the dancing, and we also introduced a raffle. We also decided to continue the practice of giving each player a personal trophy; we raised a shield (paid for by Barry Nash, who was also our first-aider) for the Clubman of the Year. The presentation of the trophies took place during the meal, between the main course and the dessert. Everybody involved in the running of the club voted on who would receive the shield as Clubman of the Year, and the winner was selected for his or her contribution to the club over the year.

The first winner to have their name engraved on the shield was a player, Brandon Cook, who incidentally was Margaret's protégé, as she had introduced him to the game. He would hold the shield for a year and then would be presented with a small replica, suitably engraved, to keep. Also one of our regular supporters presented us with a sum of money to purchase extra trophies to present to the 'Most Valuable Player of the Year on Offense and Defense' and also the 'Most Promising Rookie'.

During the close season we had to ensure that players' registrations were in place, as naturally we lost players but enrolled others. We also laid down a rule that players could not wear their names on the game shirts, because it would mean that if a player left we would lose a shirt, and it was made clear that game shirts and pants were the property of the club. This meant that we had to distribute the gear before the game and collect it afterwards. This became a hallmark of the Pioneers, with the players' shirts and pants being hung up in the changing rooms before every game. It fell to Margaret and me to wash the kit after every game, which settled what I would be doing on Mondays. We did try having the kit washed commercially, but found that any grass stains were not removed; so, as stated, it was down to us, and because of the nature of the game Margaret used to have all the repairs on shirts and pants to do. I remember after one particular game which was a mud bath, I had to spend about three hours scrubbing the pants in the bath before we could put them in the washing machine!

Another task I took on was the respraying of the helmets, as they tended to come in a variety of colours, and our colour was silver. I managed to do a deal with our local model shop to buy aerosols of the paint in bulk at a very good discount. I also contacted a firm in Norfolk to have decals for the helmets printed. These were of the team logo and we also had a three-inch-wide stripe made up of ½-inch black strips on each side, then ½-inch clear strips and a red centre strip one-inch wide to go from front to back of the helmet. At one point, I had about eight or more helmets hanging on the clothes line, drying.

During the season we had been trying to nurture the feeling of camaraderie among the supporters to form a supporters' club. So far results were not very encouraging, but we were not too worried and would try even harder in the coming seasons.

Also this was the time when we had to arrange venues for training, as sometimes the field was unavailable because of use by the soccer club. Actually, as time went on we found it necessary to take training out of town completely, as I will explain later.

## *1989*

Once more it was Super Bowl time, and Trina Collins managed to arrange, for those interested, the event at a sports club in Stacey Bushes. The club supplied a large television screen, and there were also drinks and snacks laid on – altogether a very rewarding evening.

We usually received our fixture list for the coming season in February, then it was a case of organising ambulances for home games, venues for home games if our usual pitch was unavailable, and coaches for away games, and sorting out any late registrations. One of the main problems in the early years was that we were in a different league every season, and this year it was the CGL, Combined Gridiron League, we also had a different Head Coach every season; this did not bode well for continuity of training.

At the beginning of the year there was a Super Bowl draw arranged by Living Well Health and Leisure in conjunction with the *Milton Keynes Mirror*. The draw took place in early January, and one of the players and I were present at the draw. All of the competition entries were put into a football helmet and the player with me drew the winning ticket, and we were very surprised and pleased that the winner was one of our players. The prize was a week in Miami for two and included free tickets to the Super Bowl. The organisers were very thoughtful and said that they would not publish the winner's name until he returned, so that people wouldn't know his house was empty. With the promotion of the team in mind, I went round to see the player, who was our own Tony 'Snake-hips' Jordan, and presented him with a Pioneers T-shirt with the request that he wore it at the Super Bowl game. On his return he assured me that he had worn it and that the game was everything they claimed.

I had been touting around to try and persuade some of the local businesses to advertise in our programmes with a modicum of success. However, when I approached the managing director of

Cowley and Wilson, who if you remember had previously sponsored the Bucks, he was not impressed, as he said he had had a nasty experience with American Football regarding the Bucks. I tried to convince him that everything was different now as it was all under new management. Eventually he agreed to take a full-page advert for £250 per issue, which meant five payments, one for each of the home games. All this was dependent on his being satisfied with the presentation. Unfortunately, in the first issue I made the mistake of putting his advert on the wrong page. He required it on the facing page as you opened the programme. I apologised profusely but he would not pay for that first advert. All the rest were all right, as I made sure the advert was on the correct page for the rest of the season. Other firms that I managed to persuade to advertise were some small local companies like Zenith Windows, G M Fluid Power, Milton Keynes Rewinds, D C Hall and Trusthouse Forte. All in all a very rewarding effort.

After our success last year with the Mayor's Parade, we decided to enter again. This time we put a lot of thought into how to decorate the float. The theme we decided on was 'Hands across the sea'. One of our lady supporters agreed to be dressed up as Britannia, so we dressed her in a long dress and I made a shield with a wooden frame covered by a sheet of aluminium with the Union Jack wrapped around it. Then we made a trident out of wood, and then came the helmet, which we fashioned out of card. We were then wondering how to make the plume on top of the helmet when someone had a brilliant idea. We had made a slot from two pieces of card across the top of the helmet, we then threaded the lady's hair (which was long and curly) through the slot, and it looked exactly like plumage. Now it was the turn of the Statue of Liberty. We managed to persuade one of our cheerleaders to take the part, and we started by draping her in a white sheet. The torch was made from a cut down kitchen pestle with a cardboard cut-out fence, and the flame was a wad of cotton wool stiffened with gold paint. The book was cut from a lump of wood, which was shaped, sprayed and the words added. Then came the headpiece. This we again fashioned out of card, and the final assembly was sprayed silver. We also involved Brian Day by dressing him up as a backwoodsman complete with a musket (made out of wood) and a Davy Crockett hat with a tail.

On the lorry we used some green cloth to simulate the sea, and hung a cut-out of a pair of hands in a handshake from the roof. One problem that emerged was that our Statue of Liberty had difficulty holding the torch aloft during the parade, so we tied her wrist to the roof of the lorry. Then, halfway round the course, we had to let her sit down due to travel sickness, so I told the crowd to take a good look, as this would be the only time they would ever see the Statue of Liberty sitting down. We were very pleased with our efforts, and the mayor was heard to comment that a lot of thought had gone into the entry, but we still didn't win the prize.

There is one person who I would like to bring to your attention who always said that he wouldn't sponsor us, but nevertheless gave us a terrific amount of support. This person is Mr Derek Austin, Margaret's boss. As I said he wouldn't give us cash but he allowed us to store the goalposts at his farm, and he used to allow us the use of his pickup truck with no charge. When we bought two bleachers from Upper Heyford Air Force Base he loaned us two lorries with their drivers to collect them and made no charge whatsoever; he also allowed Margaret to receive telephone calls on behalf of the club, and photocopy club paperwork such as minutes of meetings, etc., and generally assist us in any way he could. This support was ongoing throughout our involvement with the club.

Our fixture list for the season looked pretty demanding, with ten games, five home and five away to teams like Colchester Gladiators, Swindon Steelers, Coventry Bears, Cambridge Crunchers (formerly Cambridge County Cats) and Oxford Bulldogs. As you can see, Cambridge had changed their name just to suit a sponsor. This I vowed I would never do as I feel that by doing so you lose your credibility; and incidentally Cambridge reverted back to their old name as the sponsor pulled out after only one season.

We now had another new Head Coach, Howard Westervelt by name, and as you will come to see it was a mistake that would drain our resources; but more of this later.

However, before the season started we had lined up four preseason games, the first of which was against the Bedford Stags at Manor Fields. The conditions were extremely heavy, which made things difficult for both sides. The Stags opened the scoring with a touchdown but failed on the point after attempt: 0–6. The Pioneers replied by catching one of their players in the end zone for a two-point safety: 2–6. Then Ray Hunt scored his first touchdown for the Pioneers to lift the score to 8–6. The Stags managed another touchdown before Danny McAnuff ran in to score in the final minute of the game, so the Pioneers won by a very narrow margin: 14–12.

The second clash was against the Rockingham Rebels, also at Manor Fields, in improved weather conditions. The Pioneers kicked off but were unable to move the ball. Both sides exchanged punts and it was the Rebels who were the first to score with a quarterback sneak plus the point after to open the scoring: 0–7. Neither side could move the ball effectively until the second quarter, when the Rebels' quarterback again showed his pace to score, but failed with the point after: 0–13. They continued to show good form, and to pile on the agony they kicked a field goal to increase their lead to 0–16 at the half.

After the break, the Pioneers started with a pinpoint bomb from the quarterback, Simon Sparkes, to Danny McAnuff who, following a superb block by Stuart Eccles, scampered the length of the field to score: 6–16. In the fourth quarter, Simon Sparkes connected with Eif Williams for the touchdown but no point after to finalise the score at 12–16. The Pioneers had an excellent chance to go ahead when Tom Cregg, who became a father this week, caught the Rebels' punter, but the Pioneers were unable to capitalise. With time running out the Pioneers fumbled, leaving them no chance of victory.

For the next preseason we were supposed to play the St Albans Kestrels, but they were unable to make the fixture so we managed to arrange a game with the Ealing Eagles. The first quarter saw the Eagles open the scoring with a touchdown and the extra two points 0–8, but it wasn't until the second quarter that the Pioneers, after good work by Tony Jordan and Matt Eden, found themselves on the Eagles two-yard line, from where Danny Carnegie bulldozed his way over the line to make it 6–8 at the half.

After the break, the Eagles increased the pressure and scored two touchdowns to bring the score up to 6–20. It was late in the game that Simon Sparkes threw a long bomb to Danny McAnuff, only for him to catch it out of bounds. So Simon threw him another, which this time he caught in bounds and scored. Then Simon Sparkes threw a pass to Eif Williams for the two points, making the final score 14–20.

The last of our preseasons was against the Kent Rams, where the Pioneers crashed to a heavy defeat. The Pioneers were soon struggling as the defense failed to gain any consistency. With quarterbacks Butch Peddle and Matt Eden both injured, Simon Sparkes started at quarterback. Although there was a lot of energy spent, little progress was made and Kent was the first to get on the score board with a touchdown and two extra points: 0–8. They soon added another six points when Kent broke through the defense: 0–14. With a mixture of questionable refereeing and lacklustre defense, the Pioneers continued to struggle. Towards the end of the first half, the Rams went further ahead with one more touchdown making it 0–20.

The second half started just as badly for the Pioneers, as a pass from Jeff Thomas was intercepted and run back for the score; the extra two points were added, making the score 0–28. Despite desperate efforts during the rest of the third quarter and all through the fourth quarter, the Pioneers were unable to make any variation to the score, and the match finished 0–28.

Before the season proper started, the *Milton Keynes Mirror*, one of our local papers, arranged an event at Willen Lake where they were releasing a lot of balloons in a balloon race for charity. We were invited to put on a scrimmage to entertain the people. The lads were not in their kit, as it was just a bit of fun, and Howard Westervelt supplied the drinks, so no one was disappointed and we all enjoyed the break.

We now prepared to meet the Colchester Gladiators in our first regular season game by travelling to Clacton and a pitch that resembled a dust bowl. The journey to Clacton turned out to be very amusing. Margaret was in charge of the coach taking the players and some supporters. She also had the only map showing the location of the ground. I was driving my estate car loaded with the equipment, and I was followed by at least four other vehicles. Our convoy was well ahead of the coach and I had to answer the call of nature. We were on the A12 and I spotted a public convenience and turned off the road, imagine my surprise when the other drivers did the same. Unfortunately, while we were stationary the coach went past, so we had to tear up the road at 85 mph to try and catch it up. We managed to catch them just before they turned off the main road, so everything turned out OK as we followed them to the ground.

It was a disastrous start for the Pioneers as the Gladiators, who were fielding two American players, ran rings round our defense. It was a tale of missed tackles as time and again the Americans combined to outwit the defense and pile on the points making it 0–28 at half-time.

In the second half, things continued badly. Silly mistakes, fumbled tackles and bad breaks continued to punish the Pioneers, and it wasn't until late in the fourth quarter that the Pioneers' supporters had something to cheer about. Adrian Greaves took off on a fifty-seven-yard run into the end zone to score his first touchdown for the club, only to have it cancelled out for a holding penalty. However, the Pioneers were determined to restore a little pride and this they did by scoring from a seventeen-yard pass. It saved the ignominy of a whitewash and the final score was 6–47.

Next we had our first home game against the Swindon Steelers, and this time we were determined to do a lot better than before. The Steelers kicked off and the Pioneers were soon in trouble as the ball was fumbled, but the defense held well and forced Swindon to go for a field goal, but it sailed wide. The Steelers were pinned down on their two-yard line with their running backs in the end zone. After the snap the Pioneers, Perry Coultrup assisted by Doug Smith, caught their player in the end zone for a two-point safety: 2–0. The ball changed hands many times, and Wayne Eaton's punt returns were electrifying but did not produce any change to the score. In the second quarter, both sides dug in and a fifty-five-yard interception by Dave Green looked like extending the score, but the effort was nullified by a clipping penalty by Perry Coultrup. So the half-time score stayed at 2–0.

In the third quarter, the Pioneers began to show their potential and always looked like scoring, which they finally did with a dash from the thirty-yard line by Bip Holland, after the hand off by Simon Sparkes. The point after was added by Denzil Hottinger making it 9–0. The Pioneers continued to dominate in the fourth quarter when Ken LeMay intercepted the ball and it was returned to the four-yard line, from where it was run in by Tony Bayne for the score: 15–0. The final score came when a Pioneers punt by Pat McCarthy was fumbled by the Steelers on the four-yard line and recovered by the Pioneers Ken Lemay. From the four yards out, Theo Hall took the ball over the line for six points, and a pass to Stuart Eccles in the end zone added the two points. Final score: 21–0.

As a bit of a welcome break the Sports Council organised an event in Middleton Hall in Milton Keynes City Centre. This involved a lot of stalls for various organisations, including the Pioneers, but also a demonstration by the team of their callisthenics and playing skills. Robert Wade, one of our players, gave a commentary on the reasons for the various exercises and also explained the different plays as they were performed. The Trailblazers also gave a demonstration of their dance routines and performed several of their chants; they also involved any of the young ladies in the audience who wished to have a go. When we had completed our slot, the people from the sports council stall congratulated the boys and girls on their performance and pointed out that we had drawn the biggest crowd of the afternoon.

It was now our turn to meet the Coventry Bears in a tight and dour match which saw both sides very evenly matched. The ball changed hands many times but the respective defenses held and there was no score in the first half.

The second half was a repeat of the first, with neither side looking like scoring. Two long runs from the Bears caused a few anxious moments but the defense held out. It wasn't until the fourth quarter that the Pioneers broke through. Matt Eden passed the ball to Tony Jordan in the end zone and Denzil Hottinger kicked the point after, which turned out to be crucial: 7–0. Late in the period an overthrown pass was intercepted by the Bears and run in for the score, but the two-point after-attempt was thwarted leaving the final score 7–6.

The Pioneers maintained their winning streak with a game against the Cambridge Crunchers. On a blazing hot day, both defenses showed good form and it wasn't until the second quarter that either team scored. The Crunchers were the first on the board with six points but no extras: 0–6. The reply was decisive. After a good drive led by Matt Eden, he found Tony Jordan in the end zone, and Bip Holland added the extra two points, with him high-stepping into the end zone: 8–6. The Pioneers regained possession of the ball and Denzil Hottinger slotted the ball through the uprights for a field goal from thirty-five yards to increase the Pioneers' score to 11–6 at the half.

The second half was a tense defensive battle, with the offensive and defensive lines playing some excellent ball. In the fourth quarter, Cambridge came on strong, and with third and inches to go, they tried an option pass, but were stopped well short of the first down. Again the Pioneers failed to move the ball, and with little time remaining Cambridge threatened. They launched a long pass, and there was Dougie Smith to intercept. The Pioneers were then quite content to run out the clock to record their third consecutive win. Final score: 11–6.

This being a bank holiday, we were invited to take part in a spectacular at the Milton Keynes Bowl on the Monday. The show was *The Record Breakers*, featuring Roy Castle, and we were invited to put on a demonstration match against the Herts Phantoms. As the *Guinness Book of Records* was going to be there, we decided to try and get in the book with a sixteen-man press-up. Let me explain. The idea was that sixteen players would lay face down forming a circle. They would then put their legs on the previous man's shoulders, and on the command 'lift' they would all extend their arms in a press-up, so that the whole circle was supported on their arms. Unfortunately we could not find an adjudicator to verify our attempt, so we had to abandon the idea.

The game itself was well received by the crowd, with quite a big percentage of those present coming to watch; unfortunately, I cannot remember the score but I'm sure that both teams justified their inclusion in the afternoon's entertainment. Our cheerleaders, the Trailblazers, put on a dance routine which the crowd loved, so all in all it was not a bad day, and at least it got the team noticed in spite of everything else that was going on.

The game against the Oxford Bulldogs saw the Pioneers slump to their second defeat. They started strongly, but it wasn't long before the Bulldogs gained the upper hand. They opened the scoring with a completed pass for six points and also added the extra two points: 0–8. Oxford continued to press and the same combination worked together and enabled them to extend their lead to 0–14, where it remained till half-time.

The second half saw the Bulldogs keep up the pressure, and despite some dynamic running by Tony Jordan and Bip Holland the Pioneers were unable to break through. Time and again they tried but the Oxford defense held firm. With seconds remaining in the game, two strong runs by Danny Carnegie took the Pioneers to the one-yard line, but before they could convert time expired, leaving them the losers by 0–14.

We now travelled to Swindon for the return match against the Steelers, where we hoped to repeat the success we had at the first match. With many of our regular squad unavailable through injury or other commitments, the Pioneers struggled from the word go. A punt was snapped over the head of the kicker and the ball fell to Swindon close to the line. Despite a valiant attempt, the Pioneers were unable to stop the Steelers scoring the touchdown, but denied them the point after: 0–6. With the offense struggling, it wasn't long before the Steelers scored again and added the two points making it 0–14, where it remained until half-time.

After the break, the game became a mixture of farce and stupidity, as some controversial calls by the officials made the game a very scrappy affair. Neither side looked like doing anything as penalty flags were thrown all over the pitch. A very disappointing game, and it left the Pioneers 3–3 on the season.

It was now our turn to travel to Coventry to play the Bears in the return match. We had beaten them by the narrowest of margins the last time we met, and we were prepared to do it again. The first half was a battle with neither side gaining the upper hand. In the second quarter, the Bears' quarterback was sacked, causing him to fumble the ball, Victor Jolliffe recovered the ball and ran it back for a touchdown, but alas it was called back for a clipping penalty, so the first half remained scoreless.

The second half was a mirror version of the previous half, with both teams being unable to break through. It wasn't until late in the final period that the decisive score came. The Bears were being pushed back further and further by penalties towards their own end zone. The ball was on the Bears' two-yard line when the centre snapped it to the quarterback who was in the end zone, and Des James broke through and sacked him for the two-point safety: 2–0. The Pioneers held on to record a very close win, which now put them 4–3 on the season and kept them in the play-off hunt.

At home again to play the Cambridge Crunchers in the eighth game of the season, and we needed to win to stay in with a chance of the play-offs. The Pioneers started brightly with Tony Jordan and Bip Holland in fine form. However, the defenses held firm and the first quarter was scoreless. The second quarter saw the first points of the game when the Crunchers were going for a punt, and the ball was snapped too high and rolled out of the end zone for the two-point safety: 2–0. With little time left in the half, the Pioneers attempted a field goal. The kick was blocked and a Cambridge player took off looking for a certain touchdown. Bip Holland took off after him and not only succeeded in catching him but also stripped the ball to keep the Pioneers in the hunt.

If the first half belonged to the Pioneers then the second belonged to the Crunchers. In the third quarter, our quarterback, Butch Peddle, threw an interception, which Cambridge ran in for six points: 2–6. Despite the efforts of the Pioneers running backs, the Cambridge defense held firm and in the final period the offense added a touchdown pass and a two-point conversion to make the full time score 2–14.

It was with a slight feeling of apprehension that we prepared for the Colchester Gladiators in the penultimate game of the season, as the last time we'd met they completely dominated the game.

From the kick-off the Gladiators' American quarterback showed his match winning superiority against a very determined Pioneers' defense. The team managed to restrict their running back, from the New York Giants, to only thirty-four yards rushing. The Gladiators opened the scoring early in the first quarter with a touchdown from seven yards, but the two-point conversion was blocked: 0–6. The next touchdown came from a quarterback sneak plus two extra points: 0–14. The second quarter saw another successful touchdown including the point after to make it 0–21 at the half.

In the third quarter, the Pioneers managed to restrict Colchester to a touchdown plus the PAT, plus a field goal: 0–31. Then in the final period the Pioneers' defense again held Colchester to a final touchdown and added point to make the final score 0–38. This result was a slight improvement on the previous meeting's score. Now for the final game of the regular season against the Oxford Bulldogs, and the Pioneers were out for revenge at being beaten at the last encounter. The Pioneers elected to receive, and on their opening drive marched down to the Bulldogs' two-yard line, from where Danny Carnegie rushed over the line for the touchdown, no point after: 6–0. Oxford's reply was swift and decisive, with them driving downfield and scoring: 6–6. The second quarter saw the Pioneers' offense in great form. They once again drove down to Oxford's two-yard line, and this time it was Tony Jordan who carried the ball over. The point after kick was successful, bringing the score at half-time to 13–6.

The second half started with Oxford fired up, and after a fine drive they scored again but failed on the two-point attempt: 13–12. The Pioneers were not to be intimidated and replied with another score by Tony Jordan, and the extra point was added: 20–12. However, before the end of the quarter the Bulldogs gained one more touchdown with no point after, making the score 20–18. In the final quarter, Oxford scored again to lead for the first time: 20–24. The Pioneers then went to town and scored two more touchdowns with no added points: 32–24. In the dying seconds of the game, the Bulldogs were on their own ten-yard line. The quarterback stood back in the shotgun position and when the ball was snapped it sailed over his head into the end zone and was recovered by Tom Cregg for a touchdown making the final score 38–24.

So we finished the season with five wins and five losses, not bad as teams were improving all the time. We also finished the season without a Head Coach, as I will now explain.

Going back to the Howard Westervelt saga, we had agreed to pay him £500 for the season. Unfortunately he did not execute his duties to our satisfaction, so we sacked him in mid-season. He let us down on numerous occasions by not turning up for training sessions and even missing some games. As we had already paid him £250 we withheld the balance. He then took out a summons against us for the outstanding money, and I ended up in the small claims court. On the day I attended court, armed with sworn affidavits from players and staff confirming Westervelt's negligence, I was almost ignored by the registrar who claimed that all the paperwork I had was hearsay. I tried to convince him that what I had was completely relevant but to no avail, as he was biased in favour of Westervelt, and we were obliged to pay the outstanding amount, which as you can imagine took a fair slice of our funds. Needless to say, that was the last we saw of Westervelt.

Once again we were privileged at Wembley to witness this game that we had adopted being played at the highest level by greatly experienced professionals. This time it was the turn of the Eagles and the Browns, who played before a crowd of very knowledgeable fans – 73,667, such was the growing popularity of the game. The Eagles were the winners in a very close game with a scoreline of 17–13. Incidentally, one year (I'm not sure which) on the Saturday there was a soccer game billed as England against the rest of the world. The attendance was in the region of 65–70,000, and a massive police presence. On the Sunday was the American Bowl, with an attendance of 70,000 plus, and hardly a policeman in sight!

Following the end of the regular season we were invited to play a friendly game against the Russelsheim Crusaders from Germany. It transpired that the town of Rugby was twinned with this German town, and they were on a goodwill visit. Normally the game was played with Northants Storm, but as they were unavailable we were invited to take their place. The game was to be played at the Long Buckby Rugby Club. We turned up and found that the Germans didn't have a full squad, so in the interest of the sport we loaned them two of our players who, despite the language barrier, had a wonderful time. The game was an unqualified success and great fun was had by all, and with the scoreline of 27–6 to the Pioneers not reflecting the intensity of the game. After the match we were all treated to a very tasty meal in the clubhouse and the opportunity to chat to some of the German team who could speak English. Altogether it turned out to be a very interesting afternoon.

It was also during this season that Don Markham of Northants Storm approached us suggesting a merger. He said that he was prepared to move his team to Milton Keynes, and that the management set-up would remain the same. After much deliberation and consultation with the players it was decided to reject the proposal. Mr Markham was another person who, like Radcliff Philips, thought he owned a team, when in fact all he owned was a name. After this episode Mr Markham returned to the United States and the Northants Storm came under new management.

In November, we were lucky to sign up a player from Switzerland, namely James Ganter, who played for Switzerland's Bulach Giants, and it was hoped that he would bring some expertise to the team. We also signed a new Head Coach, whose name was quite well known in football circles. It was Kurt Smeby, and once again we were taken for a ride as you will find out.

Our annual Dinner and Dance was once again a great success, and our Clubman of the Year this time was Les Taylor, a very reliable supporter who we felt deserved the recognition.

## *1990*

We still managed to keep sufficient interest in the Super Bowl for us to arrange a get-together and this year we were at the rugby club in Greenleys. Among the people present, apart from our team members, were some of the rugby club management and players, who had expressed an interest in the game, which made it all the more interesting for us.

Once again we were in a different league and this year it was the NCMMA (National Conference Media and Marketing Association).

Before the regular season began we decided to arrange a game against the Belfast Spartans. I contacted their Head Coach, Stuart Smith, and we arranged the details. I managed to organise accommodation for the Irish team at a very nice hotel where I had an understanding with the manager. The hotel was on the banks of Willen Lake in a very picturesque setting.

At that time the Development Corporation were in charge of the Milton Keynes Bowl, so I approached a Mr Norman Jennings, who was in charge, and his assistant Mr Dave Hall, to ask for their assistance in promoting the match. Their response was overwhelming. They let us use the Bowl for free, and they also paid for the coach to collect the Belfast Spartans from Luton Airport, and booked it for two days so that we could return them to Luton on the Sunday. They arranged for a beer tent and a cherry picker for us to film the game. We also wanted to provide a play-bus for the kiddies, so I telephoned the mayor, Councillor Roger Bristow, to ask if he knew where we could hire a bus from; he said he would make enquiries and call me back. This he did about twenty minutes later and said that the only one he could find was in Harlow, and they wanted £250. I said that considering what the corporation were doing perhaps the council would consider paying for the play-bus.

There was a very pregnant pause and finally he agreed that the council would pay. I also asked the mayor if he would like to start the game for us, to which he agreed.

We had advertised this as an international match and a fun day out for the family. Some of the attractions we managed to organise included; a pipe band and dancers, a display of new cars by Bletchley Motors, vintage army vehicles, restored fire engines, bouncy castle, play bus, refreshments, kiddies' funfair and lots more.

The other thing I wanted to do was to alert the population of the city as to what was going on, I therefore contacted the Sealed Knot (an organisation which re-enacts olden-day battles), and arranged for them to bring a cannon and a musket. Some members of the council expressed some concern over the proposed arrangements, but I said that I felt that the population of Milton Keynes needed something like this to try and dispel the apathy which it seemed surrounded sport in the city.

We positioned the cannon and musket on top of the banking, on the left hand side of the Bowl, well away from the spectators, and then I outlined my plan. I said to the chap in charge, 'Keep your eye on the man in the light grey suit, he's the mayor, and he is going to signal the start of the match by dropping his arm. When he does, you fire the cannon, and then fire the musket every time we score a touchdown.'

The timing was perfect. As the mayor dropped his arm they fired the cannon. I hadn't realised that from the time he pulled the trigger to when the shell exploded was about ten seconds, and just as the player's foot touched the ball there was this almighty explosion, and everybody jumped in surprise, I imagined that people probably thought the IRA had moved in!

The game progressed very well with the spectators appreciating the level of dedication shown by the players on both sides, and as the Pioneers won the game 56–0, you can imagine that there were quite a few bangs that afternoon. The most disappointing thing about the whole afternoon was the poor attendance, as only about 300 people turned up. This was probably due to the fact that we had to play the game at lunchtime on the Saturday, as the Irish team had to leave fairly early on the Sunday, and people were still doing their shopping or having lunch; still, it was an experience which those who watched appreciated. Now for a résumé of the game.

When the game began the Pioneers got off to a flying start with Simon Sparkes, who made a concerted effort to score with a three-yard run: 6–0. The Pioneers continued to play impressive football with Dean Harding kicking a twenty-nine-yard field goal to raise the score to 9–0. Tony Jordan, who ran for a total of ninety-seven yards, was next on the scoresheet when he produced a snaking twenty-five-yard run for the Pioneers to take a 15–0 lead. In the second quarter, our American quarterback, Jon Carter, scored his first touchdown on British soil following a four-yard pass from fellow quarterback Simon Sparkes: 21–0. The scoring continued apace with Tony Jordan adding his second touchdown and Pete Fiala adding the two points after: 29–0. The last touchdown of the first half came when Jason Good intercepted a Belfast pass and returned it nineteen yards to make the half-time score 35–0.

It was during half-time we decided to have a bit of fun at the expense of our secretary, Dave Sparkes. He was manning the camera, and was at the top of the cherry picker, so during the break we switched off the electrics and went off with the key. He was not a happy bunny, but I must say he took it all in good part.

The third quarter saw the Pioneers experimenting and still managing to add a further seven points with Tony Jordan scoring his third touchdown and Dean Harding scoring the extra point: 42–0. The final period saw both teams tiring, but Adrian Greaves scored from three yards and Pete Fiala added the two extra points: 50–0. In the dying second, Steve Donegal caught an interception and ran for thirty-seven yards to bring the final score to 56–0. Altogether a very satisfying afternoon's work.

On the Sunday we arranged a guided tour of Milton Keynes, and the mayor said he would be honoured to conduct the tour; this was despite the fact that he had his leg in plaster! It all worked out very well, and we were surprised at how much of the city's history Roger knew. However, all the lads were really interested in was which pubs were open! Still, it was very entertaining.

Regarding the provision of a ground of our own, the council offered us three possible sites. Two were unsuitable owing to the proximity of housing, the third was OK, so I went ahead and made a model of how we proposed to lay out the field. The proposed area was huge, and if planning permission were granted it meant that the club would be responsible for the development. This set us thinking that if all went well we could set up an American Sports Centre, as well as American Football we could include Baseball and Basketball on an outside pitch. There followed a meeting with representatives of the council, and eventually I was told that we would not get planning permission as they (the council) felt that it was still too close to housing because of possible noise. The nearest housing was about a quarter of a mile away, which shows the way our councillors think. But this was not to be the end of our endeavours.

Prior to a preseason match, the Pioneers received an award from BAFRA, the British American Football Referees Association. The award consisted of a certificate and plaque, and was in recognition of the Pioneers' chain crew. The referees had voted them the top team in the UK and their award will be displayed with pride.

The Pioneers showed their potential in a hard fought preseason match against the Oxford Saints. The first two plays ended in punts as the teams sounded each other out, but from then the Pioneers tended to dominate the game. The first score came from an eighteen-yard pass from Simon Sparkes to Danny McAnuff in the end zone; they went for the two-point conversion but failed: 6–0. With the Saints deep in their own half the Pioneers' defense forced a safety from a fumbled snap: 8–0. The Saints seemed unable to move the ball with any conviction and the Pioneers were once more close to Oxford's end zone. It was fourth down and about seven yards and the Pioneers elected to go for a field goal. Dean Harding took the kick from twenty-two yards out and succeeded making the half-time score 11–0.

The second half saw the Saints try very hard but the Pioneers' defense was too strong for them. On a subsequent play Simon Sparkes once more connected with Danny McAnuff for the touchdown, and Paul Harvey kicked for the extra point: 18–0. In the final quarter, Simon Sparkes and Danny McAnuff once more combined with a scoring catch, with Paul Harvey adding the extra point. Final score: 25–0.

The following preseason game was against the Redditch Arrows and unfortunately I have no paperwork on this or the final preseason game, except to say that we did win both of them.

We then embarked on the season proper, with an opening match against the Essex Buccaneers. Despite a spirited performance, the Pioneers were unable to repeat their previous success, as you will see.

With our new American quarterback, Jon Carter, the Pioneers started well but couldn't put the finishing touches to their drives. Essex stunned everybody with a magnificent eighty-eight-yard touchdown but failed to make the conversion: 0–6. Passes were agonisingly close but just failed to connect. Essex then found the defense wanting once more, allowing them to add eight more points to their score: 0–14. The Pioneers at last woke up and following good work by the offense Tony Jordan dashed into the end zone to put six points on the board: 6–14. In the second period, the Pioneers continued to find life difficult. Essex played well and added a further six points to make it 6–20 at the half.

The third quarter was a disaster for the Pioneers as Essex added fourteen more points without reply: 6–34. The Pioneers saved their best for the final quarter, when Wayne Eaton chased the Essex quarterback all the way back to his own ten-yard line for a massive loss, and in doing so he came away with a piece of the quarterback's shirt as a souvenir. The snap, for the punt, went over the punter's head. He kicked it away, which earned him a penalty and gave the Pioneers good field position on the one-yard line. After two abortive attempts the Pioneers finally managed, through Adrian Greaves, to get the ball over the line: 12–34. Then with nothing to lose they went for the two-point conversion and were successful with Pete Fiala's catch to make the final score 14–34.

The next game was against the Colchester Gladiators at home, and a superior team comprehensively defeated the Pioneers. In the first quarter, both sides were involved in a dour struggle for dominance, and neither side looked like scoring. In the second quarter, the Gladiators stepped up the pressure by opening the scoring with a fine run. They attempted to kick for the extra point, and it was this that led to the Pioneers' only score. The kick was charged down and the Pioneers' Steve Donegal scooped up the ball and returned it ninety-three yards for a two-point safety: 2–6. Colchester then added a further six points to make the half-time score 2–12.

Disaster struck almost immediately from the second half kick-off. The Gladiators received the ball and returned it for a touchdown: 2–18. They then went into overdrive and added a further thirty-four points in the third and fourth quarters. The Pioneers changed their quarterback, and he started to move the ball. However, with only seconds to go he threw an interception, which killed the game: 2–52. This was a very disappointing performance and we needed to do better in future.

We now had to travel to Clacton for the return match against the Gladiators. Things did not start too well, as Colchester struck before the Pioneers were settled. They gained fourteen quick points, but the Pioneers refused to lie down. Jon Carter marched the Pioneers downfield and completed a pass to Pete Fiala in the end zone to open their own account: 6–14. The Pioneers continued to fight but struggled against the superior running of Colchester as they added two more touchdowns: 6–28. With Jon Carter at the helm the Pioneers battled their way to the Colchester three-yard line, from where Tony Jordan, playing his usual tireless running game, danced his way to a touchdown, and he also added the two points, to make the half-time score 14–28.

In the third and fourth quarters, Colchester proved they were the better team by increasing their score to 14–56, which included a sixty-yard touchdown run. However, the Pioneers were not to be outdone, as from the kick-off after the touchdown, Danny McAnuff received the ball on his own twenty-four-yard line, and set off like the wind, slipping tackles to complete a seventy-six-yard run for the touchdown. The final score was 20–56. This was a superb performance after the recent heavy defeat, and the Pioneers could look to improve over the next few weeks.

We now had an away match against the Oxford Bulldogs and the Pioneers opened the scoring with six points, when Simon Sparkes connected with Pete Fiala: 6–0. The rest of the quarter was scoreless as both sides fought to take control. In the second quarter, it was the Bulldogs who showed the way. The Pioneers were backed down to their three-yard line, the ball was handed off and the player was caught in the end zone for a two-point safety: 6–2. The Bulldogs continued to press and added a touchdown to make the half-time score 6–8.

The third period saw the last of the scoring as Oxford added two touchdowns with no extra points, and seemed to be coasting to an easy win: 6–20. However, the Pioneers retaliated by driving down to the two-yard line, from where Adrian Greaves took the ball and carried it swiftly over the line for six points, but Bip Holland's two-point attempt was thwarted. The fourth quarter saw more Bulldog pressure but the Pioneers' defense held firm. Final score: 12–20.

On this, a bank holiday weekend, we were up against our old rivals Coventry Bears, in a match which would show how much the team had improved. The Bears were first on the scoreboard with eight points, which was the only score in the first quarter. The Pioneers fought hard but were restricted to Dean Harding's thirty-six-yard field goal: 3–8. The Bears struck back and added a further six points to make the score at half-time 3–14.

In the second half, the Pioneers came out with all guns blazing. Jon Carter, back from injury, found receiver Ray Hunt from seventeen yards to make it 9–14. Adrian Greaves steamed in for the two points making it 11–14. The match swung again as Coventry added another six points to make it 11–20. The Pioneers pulled out all the stops, and Jon Carter sneaked in from two yards; the two points were added, making it 19–20. Coventry thought they had it sewn up in the final period when they went 19–26 up. With less than one minute to go, it looked all over for the Pioneers, who were deep in their own half. But Coventry had not reckoned with the catching ability of Danny McAnuff, and the rifle arm of Jon Carter. Jon Carter hit Danny McAnuff twice for receptions of twenty-seven yards and thirty yards to set Tony Jordan up for a three-yard touchdown to make it 25–26. The Pioneers went for the win, but Adrian Greaves was stopped on his run. The Bears killed the clock to leave it 25–26 at the end.

This was a splendid performance and augured well for the return match against Oxford.

Our next game was the return match against Oxford Bulldogs,

which we badly needed to win to salvage some of our pride. It all looked so promising when Jon Carter found Pete Fiala in the end zone from eight yards, but the attempted two-point conversion was no good: 6–0. The Bulldogs were forced to punt and the Pioneers were backed up in their own end of the pitch. Jon Carter unleashed a pass to Danny McAnuff, who set off down the pitch for a seventy-yard touchdown to make it 12–0. The Bulldogs struck back and scored a touchdown and point after: 12–7. They then came within striking distance and scored a field goal to make it 12–10 at half-time.

The Pioneers lost their way in the second half, failing to recapture their form of the previous week. Oxford, sensing victory, tightened up their defense and shut down the Pioneers' offense. They added a further six points in the third quarter to take a four-point lead. In the final period, both sides struggled for supremacy, but with numerous penalties the ball went back and forth to no avail. The Pioneers tried to move the ball but Jon Carter was brilliantly intercepted and time ran out. Final score: 12–16.

We now move on to the next game, which is the second encounter with the Essex Buccaneers. Essex took an early lead and completely dominated the first half, and although the Pioneers worked hard they had little luck and were 0–20 down at half-time.

The Pioneers came out fighting in the second half, with Jon Carter in fine form. They held the Buccaneers to a scoreless third quarter. In the fourth quarter, they were still fired up. With Jon Carter leading and Tony Jordan and Bip Holland producing some fine running, they marched down to the one-yard line. From there Tony powered in to make the score 6–20. They were unsuccessful with the two-point attempt. Essex hit back with another eight points to make it 6–28.

The Pioneers were not downhearted. Jon Carter marched his men down to the twenty-one-yard line. He took the snap and set off down the pitch for a touchdown, but failed to convert for the extra points: 12–28.

With little time remaining, the Pioneers had the ball on the one-yard line, but strong Buccaneers defense prevented any further score, making the final score 12–28.

Continuing this dreadful season, we travelled to Feltham to play the London Aces, who used to be the Heathrow Jets. The Pioneers fell to 0–8 in a match that was marred by bad refereeing. The Pioneers fielded a below strength squad and were soon behind to an Aces touchdown. Jon Carter got the team downfield within striking distance but had to be content with a thirty-eight-yard field goal. Then Jon Carter had to retire from the game with a shoulder injury. Bip Holland took over in the quarterback slot but failed to make any impression on a strong Aces defense, with the lack of numbers beginning to tell. The Aces extended their lead to 3–33 at half-time.

The second half was littered with poor refereeing; there were numerous strange decisions as the officials lost control of the game. The Aces had one player ejected for a terrible late hit and were lucky not to lose another. The only scoring in the second half came in the fourth quarter with the Aces scoring another two touchdowns, one from a run and the other from a punt return, making the final score 3–45.

In the last home game of the season, we were matched against the Walsall Titans, a team we hadn't met before. With a depleted squad the Pioneers kept pace with the Titans, making sure that the first quarter was scoreless. In the second quarter, the Titans opened the scoring with three quick breaks and led by 0–20 at half-time. The Titans were still going strong in the third quarter but the Pioneers wouldn't give up. They restricted the Titans to a fourth and long, the centre snapped the ball over the head of the kicker, and the ball rolled out of the end zone for a two-point safety for the Pioneers. The Titans put on a further twenty points to finish the game with a scoreline of 2–40. This result put the Pioneers 0–9 on the season with one match to go. We looked on this as a learning experience and were determined to do better next season. We told our supporters, 'Don't give up on us yet!'

The last match of the regular season was played on a Saturday evening in pouring rain in Coventry. The Pioneers looked bright at the start but failed to capitalise as Coventry fumbled the ball, but the offense were unable to take advantage of the mistake, and it wasn't long before the opposition were six points to the good. In the second quarter, the heavens opened, which made play difficult, but the Bears managed another score, bringing the half-time score to 0–12.

In the third quarter, despite some hard work from the Pioneers, Coventry running backs proved to be elusive, and in spite of the weather they managed to add a brace of touchdowns plus the points after to raise the score to 0–26. The Pioneers eventually started to move the ball but it was too late, so the score of 0–26 stood at the final whistle.

This was a very disappointing season for the Pioneers, but they vowed to return stronger and wiser from the experience gained this year.

Incidentally, the game we played against the Walsall Titans was marred by a show of ill feeling against our cheerleaders by the Titans' cheerleaders. I understand it all began before the game started as the girls were changing. Some of the Titans' cheerleaders locked our girls in the toilets, and one of our girls had to climb out of the window – breaking the toilet pan in the process – to get round and release the rest of the squad. There was also a lot of bad-mouthing and swearing from their squad, but our girls showed remarkable restraint by not retaliating. An official complaint was lodged with the Titans' management, and an apology was eventually forthcoming.

As you will have noted, the Pioneers ended the season losing all of their games, but I would like to put on record the fact that, although we lost every game, we managed to keep the team together to fight on for another season. We were extremely pleased that the lads put their trust in the management to carry the team on to success in the future.

I have catalogued all the American Bowl games as I feel that they did have some impact on the domestic game. This year was no exception, as the Raiders and the Saints came to visit. Unfortunately, the attendance had begun to dwindle and this year was down to 63,106. However, the game was still just as exciting and the Saints emerged the winners 17–13.

Jon Carter's mother and father, Jon Sr and Pat, arrived in the country on the Friday for a holiday, and I managed to arrange hotel accommodation for them at the local hotel, where I had previously lodged the Irish team, as I had a standing deal with the manager and got the room cheap. I went to the hotel to greet them when they arrived, and invited them out to dinner. The evening was a great success, although the Americans do tend to insist on paying for everything, and it does sometimes get a bit embarrassing. Anyhow, we got to know each other very well, so I invited them to take a trip with us to the Isle of Wight on the Sunday.

I hired a minibus from where I worked, which we picked up at six o'clock in the morning. Needless to say, Jon Sr insisted on paying for the hire of the minibus, and also the fuel, which did embarrass me a bit. However, we went home and picked up the others who were travelling with us. There were ten of us altogether, including Pat and Jon, Jon Jr, Tim Harris, one of our players, and his wife, Jocelyn, Betty and Tom, Margaret's sister and her husband, Brian Day and Margaret and myself. Incidentally, Jocelyn was pregnant, which gave rise to a bit of concern as she was sitting right at the back of the van, and was consequently being bounced around somewhat. Still, we managed to avoid any embarrassment due to Jocelyn's condition.

The journey down was a bit hectic, as we had to hurry to catch the earliest ferry possible. Jon was a bit perturbed and pointed out that they weren't allowed to do 80 mph in the States, to which I retorted we weren't in the States! The weather was very windy too, which made the crossing of the Solent a bit hair-raising. In fact, as we turned to pull into East Cowes the boat listed heavily to starboard, causing a lot of china in the galley to smash. Jon and Tim made a grab for the curtains to save themselves and ripped them down. Margaret also had to help an elderly lady who fell over, but luckily didn't hurt herself. I heard some time later that the captain had received a severe reprimand following the incident.

However, we docked safely and proceeded to explore the island, taking in as much as possible in the short time we had. We started with a visit to Osbourne House, then from there we dashed right across the island to Alum Bay, where the weather was not very kind to us as the wind had picked up to gale force, and it also started raining. The folks had decided to visit the glass works, so I said I would get the minibus and meet them outside because of the rain. In manoeuvring the bus as close to the doors as possible, I dented the side of the bus on a post. This I would have to explain when I returned the bus the following day. We then travelled back across the island and took in a couple of other points of interest, and then alas, it was time to catch the ferry back to the mainland. Happily the trip turned out to be a huge success, and I returned everybody safely home. After this little episode the Carters then went off on a tour of Europe. Incidentally, I did not get into trouble over the slight accident aforementioned.

It was this year that we gained a further prize award. We were playing in the Coca-Cola League, Division 2, and were surprised to receive the Team of the Year award from BAFA (British American Football Association), which we understood was for our conduct both on and off the pitch. This form of recognition was a very welcome boost to our morale.

It was about this time that we endeavoured to set up teams to cater for the younger members of the community. There was the Pee Wees for those aged eight to fourteen, and Juniors for fourteen- to eighteen-year-olds. Praise must go to Robert Wade, one of our players whose efforts in recruiting the youngsters were magnificent. He spent time going into schools and introducing the children to the rudiments of the game, and we were surprised when even some of the girls showed an interest. The response was good so we started training and managed to organise a few friendly games to keep the interest going. I'll have more about the progress of the minor teams later on.

Our annual general meeting was held as usual in October and there were a few changes to the positions of the committee members. Trina Collins was elected as Chairman, but still retained the post for transport/statistician. I was voted in as secretary and Andy Howe became game day manager. Andy's wife, Anita, was also called on to help with the stats. Gladstone McKenzie Sr was elected as Team Manager, Margaret was again re-elected as Treasurer, and Brian Day stayed as Programme Editor. This was how the new committee lined up for the coming year.

We held our annual Presentation Dinner and Dance again at the Woughton House Hotel. The event was well attended by members and guests, and thanks went to Trina Collins for organising the evening. The Clubman of the Year award was presented to club stalwart Andy Howe who gave invaluable service to the club.

At the end of the season, we once again signed a new Head Coach, hoping that this time we had found the right one. The man we signed was Mr George Cunningham. George was with the American Air Force stationed at Chicksands, and had been involved with British American Football since its inception; he was also a very competent commentator and a great friend.

Everybody was very surprised when George turned up for a training session with his ankle in plaster and wielding a walking stick. When asked what had happened, he looked a bit sheepish and told us that he had broken his ankle on a fishing trip. Honestly, we didn't laugh! He also brought with him four American coaches who were serving with him on the base, so we were looking for great things in the next season.

# *1991*

In January, the team were invited by Ladbrokes in the City Centre to have a bet on the outcome of the Super Bowl in the States. The teams involved were the New York Giants v the Buffalo Bills; we put £30 on Buffalo to win, with odds of 25 to 1, and if successful the money would go to Willen Hospice for terminally ill patients. The game turned out to be one of the closest ever played, with the Giants winning by just one point. However, Ladbrokes very kindly put up the £30 and added another £25 as a consolation, allowing us to present Willen Hospice with £55, a very generous gesture. Also we got the manageress to dress up in one of our cheerleader's uniforms, and she definitely looked the part.

It was time once again to announce a change of league. This year it was the NDMA (National Division Marketing Association) Coca-Cola Division 2, Northern Conference. Being sponsored by Coca-Cola meant that we had to remove the Budweiser badges from the game shirts and sew on the Coca-Cola badges. This particular chore kept Margaret busy for some time.

The first game of the season was an away match against Redditch Arrows. This was our first meeting with this team, except for a preseason back in 1990, which the Pioneers won, and they proved to be a very competent side. The game was played on a pitch next to a cemetery, so I asked everyone to keep the noise down so as not to disturb our next-door neighbours.

The first quarter was a 0–0 stalemate as both teams tested each other out. The Pioneers had a chance in the second quarter when they had the Arrows on their own one-yard line, but were unable to capitalise as the Arrows' defense held firm.

In the second half, it was the Arrows who opened the scoring, totally against the run of play, by making the touchdown but failing to gain the extra point: 0–6. This stung the Pioneers into action. From the kick-off they put together an impressive drive, and with Tim Harris making a superb return, they marched to the one-yard line again. This time Tony Jordan, watched by his six-month-old son, Bradley, bulldozed his way into the end zone. The Pioneers went for the point after but the kick was too low, making the score to 6–6. However, disaster was to strike. After a penalty caused the ensuing kick-off to be retaken, the Arrows returned the ball eighty-seven yards for the touchdown and the two-point conversion was good. Final score: 6–14.

On the Sunday we left Milton Keynes at about 8.30 a.m. to make the journey to Bolton for our next game.

The Pioneers took the initiative from the start. Quarterback Simon Sparkes moved the ball well and hooked up with Danny McAnuff for a twenty-nine-yard touchdown, and Paul Harvey slotted the ball through the uprights for the point after: 7–0. The Buccaneers struck back immediately with their own touchdown, they went for the two-point conversion but failed: 7–6. The Pioneers were not to be denied. They marched down the field and swept into the end zone on a three-yard carry by Tim Harris, but they failed on the two-point attempt: 13–6. By now the Pioneers were really fired up. The defense refused to give up yardage and the offensive line were creating big holes in Bolton's defensive line, so it came as no surprise when Simon Sparkes once more connected with Danny McAnuff for a ten-yard touchdown pass. Tony (Snake-hips) Jordan bulldozed over the line for the two points to make it 21–6 at half-time.

There was no let up in pressure in the second half as the Buccaneers were unable to make significant progress. The Pioneers took over the ball on their own goal line, and using an impressive array of passes and runs, which gives lie to recent claims that they are not good enough for Division 2 football, they moved it the length of the field, capping it with another Danny McAnuff touchdown: 27–6. Still the Pioneers refused to let up on the pressure, with Tony Jordan scoring again to raise the score to 33–6. The final period saw the Pioneers continue their fine performance, by adding to Bolton's misery with a two-point safety following a bad snap by their centre. Final score: 35–6.

Next we had to face the Coventry Jaguars (a new name, as they used to be the Bears) in two consecutive games the first at home at Manor Fields. Coventry were ranked number one in the conference. The early plays did not show the game ahead, as both sides traded punts. However, the Jaguars soon took control and took the score to 0–22 at the end of the first quarter. The Pioneers finally got on the scoreboard in the second quarter, when Simon Sparkes found Danny McAnuff with a long pass to the two-yard line, from where Tony Jordan forced his way over the line for the touchdown, with Danny McAnuff also reeling in the catch for the two points after, to make the half-time score 8–28.

The Jaguars took total control of the second half and racked up a further twenty-two points without answer, to obliterate the Pioneers with a devastating score of 8–50.

To illustrate how problems can arise, when it came to our return match with Coventry, they had no venue, so we had to come up with a solution. We needed the game to be played.

We looked around, and one of our players, who worked at the Upper Heyford American Air Force Base, contacted the authorities and we were offered the opportunity to play at RAF Croughton, a satellite base. They said that they would mark out the pitch for us, but on arrival we found that they had marked it wrongly. They had marked it for English football, and they were Americans! We scrounged all of their lime and set to work to put it right. Unfortunately before we finished we ran out of lime, I rushed off to see if I could buy some more, but all the merchants were closed, so I ended up buying a bag of Artex from B&Q! I wonder if those lines are still there!

The Pioneers found inspiration and hope at half-time after the Jaguars had mauled them 0–48. The Pioneers won the second half 18–8, if you want to put it that way. And why not, after a brave display against Coventry! It was the most points the Coca-Cola Division 2 leaders have conceded this season. Old Snake-hips, Tony Jordan, ran twenty-eight yards for the touchdown, after an inspired team talk fired up the Pioneers at the break. The Jaguars immediately showed their claws with a touchdown and two-point conversion. But Simon Sparkes hit wide receiver Danny McAnuff with a five-yard pass to make it 12–56. Chris Carson made an interception to keep the rally going, and Tony made another touchdown from six yards to end the game 18–56. The atmosphere was great, as we had an American audience, and we surprised them with our knowledge of their national game.

It was now time for the return match against Redditch, this time at home, and we were hoping to turn the tables, but alas it was not to be. The Pioneers started brightly, restricting the Arrows' offense. At the end of the first quarter the Pioneers were on the Arrows' five-yard line. The teams changed ends, and Tony Jordan burrowed in for the touchdown; but Paul Harvey's attempt at the PAT was no good: 6–0. In the second quarter, the Arrows changed their quarterback and their fortunes by scoring two touchdowns to make the score at half-time 6–12.

After the break, the third period was scoreless, but in the final period the Arrows increased their lead to 6–18, and that was how it finished.

Next we had two games back to back with the Stoke Spitfires. The first was away, and because of difficulties with Stoke's ground we had to play on the Saturday evening. This proved to be a bit awkward for some of the players because of work commitments. However, we managed to assemble sufficient players to make the journey, and duly arrived to strut our stuff.

Stoke jumped to an early lead with a touchdown and point after to open the scoring at 0–7. Another two points were added when the snap went high over Dean Harding's head and out of the end zone for a two-point safety: 0–9. Stoke added a further seven points and the Pioneers looked a bit dispirited: 0–16. It was then that the Pioneers started to play, and after an impressive drive Tony Jordan broke through from the three-yard line to make it 6–16 at the end of the quarter.

The second quarter belonged exclusively to the Spitfires as they racked up twenty-two unanswered points to make it 6–38 at half-time.

After the break, Stoke added a further touchdown: 6–44. But the Pioneers were not entirely out of the game as they came up with another score from a seven-yard pass by Simon Sparkes to Danny McAnuff: 12–44. Then in the fourth quarter Simon Sparkes and Danny McAnuff did it again to raise it to 18–44, but alas the game finished as it started, with a Spitfire touchdown and PAT to make the final score 18–51. The

Pioneers returned home a little dispirited, but willing to take them on again at home.

The day of the home game arrived and the Pioneers were all fired up to exact revenge; however, it was not to be, as Stoke were also in fighting mood.

The game kicked off and the Spitfires scored on their first two drives to open the scoring 0–13. The Pioneers finally responded with a touchdown of their own from an eight-yard pass by Simon Sparkes, this time to Steve Green for his first touchdown for the club, and to make the first quarter score 6–13. Stoke started the second quarter as they did the first by scoring another two touchdowns: 6–26. Again the Pioneers replied with a drive, which was capped with a seventeen-yard pass to Danny McAnuff: 12–26. The Spitfires struck back to make the half-time score 12–33.

The Pioneers dominated the second half. In a fine defensive performance, the Pioneers held the Spitfires to a scoreless half and got the final points in the third quarter, when Stoke's punter was caught deep in the end zone by Tim Harris for a two-point safety. This brought the final score to 14–33. It was a loss, but the difference from the last game was significant.

We now had the return match against Bolton in our own backyard, and we were determined to redeem our pride and get back to winning ways. The Pioneers started well, and when Mark Goodier intercepted a pass it enabled Tony Jordan to run the ball in from six yards; he also ran in the two-point conversion to make it 8–0. The Pioneers dominated the second quarter. Tony Jordan made another three-yard dash to make it 14–0, but the attempted point after was unsuccessful. Mark Goodier then made his second big contribution of the half with a fumble recovery. As with his first effort, this led to another touchdown with Tim Harris scoring from one yard: 20–0. By now the Pioneers' defense were really fired up and it was Steve Donegal who fell on a fumble to set up Danny McAnuff to make an electrifying thirty-nine-yard run to raise the score to 26–0 at half-time.

The third quarter was scoreless, but was marked by a fine offensive drive by Bolton, and an equally fine display by the Pioneers' defense, stopping the Buccaneers just short of the goal line.

The fourth quarter saw the Pioneers in a dominant mood. Ray Hunt got his name on the score sheet with a twenty-yard catch to make it 32–0. The Pioneers developed a habit of turning mistakes into points. After Dean McBroom's fine interception, Steve Donegal capped an electrifying six play series with his first rushing touchdown from five yards raising the score to 38–0. Steve Green added the two points to make it 40–0. The Pioneers completed a superb performance with Tim Harris rushing in for his second touchdown of the game with a two-yard run making the final score 46–0.

Our next match was an inter-conference game against the Medway Mustangs to be played at Manor Fields. After our win the previous week the Pioneers were all fired up to try and repeat the performance.

The Pioneers started well and dominated the early exchanges. They quickly got onto the score sheet with Danny McAnuff hauling in a twenty-yard touchdown pass plus the two-point conversion by Steve Green: 8–0. In the second quarter, the Pioneers continued to show their excellent form with another touchdown, with Danny collecting another pass of twenty-six yards but no point after: 14–0. The defense then decided it was time to get in on the act, and Clive Mindham recovered a fumble and returned it twenty-one yards for the score, his first for the club. Steve Green added the two points to make it 20–0. Steve Green was celebrating again when he scooped up a twenty-three-yard pass to raise the score to 28–0 at half-time.

The second half was much the same, as Medway struggled against a tough defense. The Pioneers finally put the game out of reach in the third quarter with a six-yard touchdown by Ray Hunt, making it 34–0. The defense were having a field day by now, and in the final quarter Mark Goodier ran in an interception from thirty-three yards to wrap it up with a final scoreline of 40–0.

For the last game of the regular season we travelled to Croydon to play the SMC (South Merton and Croydon) Admirals. When we arrived at the ground we found that we had left half the game shirts behind; this discovery reduced Margaret to tears. As we were so far from home it was impracticable to attempt to go home to recover the rest of the shirts, so we went to see their officials to see if we could find a solution to the problem. They were very understanding and agreed to let us use their second strip. The ironical thing about it all was that we won the game using their shirts. The match went as follows.

The Pioneers finished the season in a blaze of glory, winning in a tense pendulum battle. It swung back and forth with both teams matching score for score. The Pioneers started slowly and SMC set up an early score: 0–6. The Pioneers rallied and started to gain momentum, and following a pitch length drive got down to SMC's two-yard line, but before they could convert they had to change ends with the end of the quarter. They did convert on the first play when Tony Jordan, playing his retirement game, powered in to even the score: 6–6. SMC struck back with a touchdown and two points to make it 6–14. The Pioneers refused to lie down, and with some solid running from Tony Jordan, they marched down the field and Simon Sparkes tossed the ball thirty-one yards to Danny McAnuff for the TD and Tony Jordan added the two points evening the score at 14–14. The game swung SMC's way again as they scored a further eight points. Despite two late catches by Steve Green, one a spectacular one-handed effort, the Pioneers were unable to score. Half-time score: 14–22.

The second half saw the Pioneers fight back, with Tony Jordan once again rushing in from one-yard to make it 20–22. The Pioneers finally got their noses in front, after the defense had held the Admirals on their own five-yard line, and were forced to punt. The ball landed in the hands of Danny McAnuff, who electrified the crowd with a dazzling twenty-seven-yard return into the end zone. Tony added his final two points of an illustrious career to make it 28–22. The Admirals, to their credit, came back to make it all square at 28–28. The Pioneers finally sealed it when Danny hauled in an eight-yard pass to make it 34–28. The last minute was a tense one as the Pioneers held their nerve, forcing SMC to throw three incomplete passes allowing the Pioneers to snatch the victory.

In his final match, Tony Jordan rushed for 143 yards. The Pioneers finish with a creditable four wins and six losses for a season which had looked to be in ruins.

The American Bowl this year featured the Bills and the Redskins and drew the lowest crowd of the year at 50,474. The game was won by the Bills 17–13. Also this year we had the initiation of NFL Europe, with England fielding a team called the London Monarchs. This team racked up an impressive tally over the season and won the right to play in the first World Bowl staged at Wembley. Their opponents on the day were the Barcelona Dragons, and Monarchs emerged the winners with a scoreline of 21–0.

It was during this year that George Cunningham, who as I have said was stationed at Chicksands, invited the whole team and their wives and girlfriends to a barbecue at the base. It was a marvellous gesture, and the lads and lasses had a lot of fun playing volleyball, basketball and generally having a great time – and a grand feast to boot. Everybody had travelled to Chicksands by coach, and the only thing that marred the day was the coach drivers' refusal to join in; however, it was all very greatly appreciated by everyone.

After much debating, we finally selected a name for our junior team; it was decided to call them the 'Mavericks' in line with the pioneering spirit that we tried to instil into our players.

It was also at the end of this season that we lost one of our best and most respected players. Mr Tony (Snake-hips) Jordan decided to retire, and as a mark of our respect we decided to retire his number as well. Tony was a dedicated player, and on two occasions he went on holiday with his family on the Saturday, and returned on the Sunday to play the game, then after the match he went back on holiday. Needless to say we were very sorry to see him go, but as he said, 'When it takes three weeks for an injury to heal, instead of three days, it's time to call it a day.' Who can argue with that?

The annual general meetings were becoming more and more difficult, as player attendance was falling off rapidly, which made it very awkward when it came to voting on relevant issues. However, there were only two major changes this time. The first one was a change of chairman, Linda Punter. The second the election of a new president, and the person elected was Bob Luddington, who was an American who had taken a great interest in the club.

Then at the end of the season George stepped down because of commitments, and once again we were looking for a new Head Coach.

Our annual Dinner Dance was once again held at the Woughton House Hotel and our guest of honour was the mayor, Roger Bristow, and his wife. Five of the lads from London decided to dress up in full Scottish regalia, which certainly added a touch of class. The procedure we had introduced at these functions was for the guest of honour to make an introductory speech; we would then have the first and main courses of the meal followed by the presentations of the trophies. On this occasion the players were being called on one at a time to collect their trophy, and when it came to the turn of one of the lads dressed in the kilt, he was making his way between the tables when someone lifted his kilt, and to the mayor's wife's embarrassment he had nothing on underneath. The hall erupted into hilarious laughter and I must say that the mayor's wife took it all in good part. The name to be engraved on the Clubman of the Year shield this year was Margaret Gifford, who as you have probably realised was a very deserving recipient.

## *1992*

Surprisingly, we were still in the same league, the Coca-Cola League, and we were looking forward to a more successful season. For our Head Coach this season we signed up Mr Bob Ludington, another American, who as we said earlier was also president of the club. He had extensive knowledge of the game and, like George, refused any payment.

This season we only had eight games and our opponents were London Olympians 2, West London Aces (formerly Heathrow Jets), Cardiff Mets and Kent Mustangs.

About this time we had a meeting at Manor Fields regarding the use of the pitch for the coming season. We were very surprised and shocked when their committee told us that they would require a substantial sum of money in advance for the season. We were not prepared to accede to their demands so we took all our equipment and left. This meant that we would have to find another venue in a hurry. I contacted the chairman of Milton Keynes Rugby Club based in Greenleys, and arranged a meeting between our respective committees. The outcome was that we would be playing our home games at Greenleys. We moved our goalposts and stored them under an outbuilding, as until we could arrange to set the bases in place we would use the rugby posts.

We arrived one evening for training, and I noticed that our goalposts were not where we had put them, so I asked if they had been moved, but on further investigation it transpired that they had been stolen! This meant that we had to acquire some new posts as soon as possible. I made a few enquiries and found a supplier based in Paignton in Devon. He agreed to supply us with posts, bases and protective pads, and would deliver them by road. All went well and I met the driver and escorted him to the field. Then came the task of digging the holes for the bases and concreting them in place. The bases consisted of a steel tube three feet long and three inches in diameter. We had to dig a hole one foot square and three feet deep, place a lump of concrete in the bottom, then insert the tube and surround it with concrete. The arrangement worked very well, as their club had three pitches and they virtually gave us one. We were responsible for the condition of the field, which is why I invested in a petrol mower, and spent many hours cutting the grass, with the assistance of some of the other dedicated helpers, to make it suitable for games.

It was at one of our evening training sessions at Greenleys that a rather bizarre incident occurred. One of our players, Eddie Manu, turned up late and I had to accompany him to the changing rooms, as I had the keys. While he was changing I was standing in the doorway talking to him when a female voice behind me said, 'Excuse me can you help me with the showers, as I can't get them to work.' I turned to give an answer, and stood there open mouthed, as the lady in question was completely naked. I swear that Eddie couldn't speak a word and just sat there absolutely gobsmacked. I eventually managed to regain control and went with her to fix the showers for her and her male partner.

We opened the season with a game against the London Olympians 2 and things started badly when our quarterback was carried off the field with a shoulder injury. Worse was to come when some strong running from London, and some amazingly inept officiating, had the Pioneers reeling with a 0–8 first quarter deficit. It got worse in the second quarter when the Olympians were deemed to have scored a safety, despite the ball being pushed out of the end zone by their players. This totally threw the Pioneers who were 0–22 down at half-time; again the referees played an unwelcome part.

The second half showed a truer picture of the teams with the Pioneers dominating the third quarter, but being unable to score. The Pioneers finally opened their 1992 account in the final quarter courtesy of a thirty-two-yard pass launched by Simon Sparkes that appeared to have been caught by two London players, but they collided and knocked the ball into the air, allowing our receiver Danny McAnuff to snap up the ball and run it in for the touchdown. Despite three attempts, due to penalties, the Pioneers were unable to add the point after, making the score

6–22. The Olympians completed the scoring with eight points to run out 6–30 winners.

Now we had to face the London Aces at home, and in the first quarter we were unable to capitalise on several drives and ended up sixteen points down at the change of ends. The Pioneers managed to stem the advance somewhat in the second period, allowing the Aces only one touchdown to bring the score at halftime to 0–22.

The third quarter saw the Pioneers overwhelmed by the Aces who racked a further twenty-four unanswered points: 0–46. In the final period, the Aces experimented with different quarterbacks. It was then that the Pioneers flexed their defensive muscle. Dave 'Basher' Watson terrorised the opposing quarterback with a total of three sacks. The Pioneers also changed their quarterback, but to no avail as the Aces added a further touchdown to end the game with a massive 0–50 scoreline.

The Pioneers had to travel to Feltham for the return match against the Aces, where they hoped they could improve on the previous result. The first quarter looked like being a repeat of the last game, with the Aces scoring fourteen points. It was in the second quarter that the Pioneers began to show their mettle, and it was not long before they broke their duck. Simon Sparkes launched a twenty-three-yard pass to Carl Appleton, who made a superb catch and ran into the end zone for six points, his first for the club. He then, with another catch, added the two extra points to make the score at half-time 8–14.

Things looked to be turning for the Pioneers but it was not to be. The Aces pulled further ahead and in the second half scored twenty-four unanswered points to bring the score to 8–38. This was a better result than last time but there is still a long way to go.

After travelling to Cardiff, the Pioneers put in another poor performance against their Welsh opponents. For the first time this season they scored first when Danny McAnuff caught a pass from Simon Sparkes to lead 6–0. They failed miserably to turn this into something positive, with poor tackling and too many intercepted passes; they trailed 6–14 at the half. Any hopes of a better second half were soon dashed as the Mets took total control of the game. They piled up the points against an ineffective defense to win 6–40.

At home against the Cardiff Mets, the Pioneers' season was effectively over with their fifth straight defeat, but they went down fighting. This was a much improved performance, as the new players began to understand what was required of them, and it augured well for the future.

The first quarter was scoreless with some excellent defensive moves by the Pioneers. The second quarter was much the same till just before half-time, when the Mets scored two touchdowns and kicked both points after: 0–14. The Pioneers were caught on the hop at the start of the second half when the Mets returned the kick-off all the way for a touchdown and the point after: 0–21. Cardiff then ran up a further fourteen points due to a lot of errors incurring a host of penalties for both teams: 0–35. In the last period, the Pioneers decided to experiment by changing the quarterback. Simon was replaced by Paul (Bear) Herbert, who was returning from injury. He handed off to Joey (DJ) Denkiewicz, the running back, who saw a gap open up and dashed forty-three yards to score his first touchdown for the club 6–35, and that was how the score remained to the final whistle.

It was now our turn to meet the Kent Mustangs for the first time and as far as we were concerned they were an unknown factor. The Pioneers managed to force a fumble, very early in the game, to gain good field position. From there Paul Herbert threw a three-yard pass to Ray Hunt for the six points. They were unable to capitalise on the advantage, and Kent went in for the score plus the two-point conversion, making the score 6–8 at the end of the quarter. Kent scored again at the start of the second period, and then proceeded to increase their points tally by a total of twenty-two points to make the half-time score 6–30.

The second half saw the Pioneers give all they had, and with the same combination of Paul Herbert and Ray Hunt they scored the second touchdown. This time the point after attempt was successful, with Paul Herbert connecting with Danny for the two points extra: 14–30. However, the Mustangs replied with a further two scores, which extended their total to 14–46.

The final period was a very ill-tempered affair, with a player from each team being ejected. The number of penalties on both teams gave up a lot of yards, but there was no further score.

The Pioneers finished their home season on a disappointing note with a second defeat by the London Olympians 2.

The Pioneers managed to contain London to a scoreless first quarter, but were unable to score themselves. In the second period, London scored two touchdowns plus one two-point conversion making the half-time score 0–14.

The third quarter saw London score twice more but only one two-point conversion: 0–28. On the following kick-off, Danny McAnuff caught the ball, and with a stunning run of seventy-six yards returned it for six points to the Pioneers. In the fourth quarter, the Olympians stretched their lead to finish the game 6–44.

During the half-time break there was a display by Milton Keynes's own marching band, the Mercury Korps. The Korps, made up of young people, were on only their third display and were well received by the spectators, and showed a lot of promise for the future.

For the final game of the regular season saw us travelling to Erith in Kent. The game resulted in another defeat marred by the awful behaviour of the Mustangs. The match had to be stopped twice as the officials tried to restore order.

The Pioneers started badly, allowing Kent to score two touchdowns, but blocked the attempted points after: 0–12. In the second quarter, the Pioneers drove down to Kent's one-yard line. On the next play they fumbled the ball; Kent picked it up and returned it for a ninety-nine-yard touchdown. Kent continued with the pressure and added a further thirteen points. It was at this point that the Pioneers gave their supporters something to shout about. Danny McAnuff caught a seventy-three-yard pass from Paul Herbert for the touchdown, then Paul Herbert himself crashed over the line for the two points, making the half-time score 8–25.

Kent added another eight points in the third quarter as the Pioneers kept their cool despite severe provocation, sending the score to 8–33. In the fourth quarter, the Pioneers attained their highest score of the season when Mark Lewis scored his first touchdown for the club with a one-yard run plus two extra points from a catch by Ray Hunt: 16–33. There was yet another delay as

Kent's discipline disappeared. This disturbed the Pioneers' concentration and they conceded a touchdown to make the final score 16–39.

It had been a disappointing season with the team losing all their games, but nevertheless the outlook for the following year was very encouraging. The team showed that although we may be winless, we were certainly not gutless. They played every game with fervour and deserved our praise for not giving up.

The American Bowl this year saw the return of the 49ers against the Redskins. This combination raised the attendance to 61,722 and the 49ers were the winners at 17–15.

We didn't sack Bob Luddington, as after all he was President, but he was as frustrated as we were and virtually sacked himself. After the final he approached us and told us he was resigning from his position of Head Coach and also the position of President. We were very disappointed at his decision, but as he said that as the team had lost every game over the season he felt that he was responsible.

Being that it was a short season, we sought to arrange a game against an American team, and clinched a meeting with the Upper Heyford Sky Kings at their base. To enhance our chances we drafted in players from Kent Mustangs and Northants Storm. The game started slowly as the lads had only been together during practice, but as the game progressed they grew more confident. The Pioneers drew first blood when a Heyford punt was charged down and returned for the score; the point after attempt was no good. This stunned the Sky Kings, as they were fielding a squad of seventy players. The game turned out to be a momentous battle and the Pioneers, to their credit, showed their mettle with a final score of 28–26 in Heyford's favour.

Another challenge that we accepted was a game that we played against another American base team from Lakenheath. We played the game at the base and unfortunately we were thrashed with a scoreline of 0–51. However, the experience was worth a lot, as we learnt a great amount regarding tactics and the execution of plays. At the end of the game we were standing at the entrance to the field. It seems that all the pitches on the bases are enclosed with a wire fence. To continue, as I said Margaret and I were standing at the gate with our sweetie jar, when a couple of the Americans walked past and one said to the other, 'There, I told you they had a sweetie jar!' – or as they put it, a candy jar.

It was during this period of poor results that the football press i.e. *First Down*, began referring to the Pioneers as the 'Whipping Boys'. These allegations were considered derogatory, and several teams rallied with us to condemn these journalists. However, it was time to prove them very, very wrong.

As I said back in 1990, we formed a junior team, which we finally named the 'Mavericks'. The Head Coach was a retired player, Bob Wade, who instilled a sense of discipline and respect among the lads. 1991, as we said, was a learning year, and as stated earlier we also managed to organise some friendlies. The Pee Wees and younger Juniors had left us and gone to Newport Pagnell, so with the older boys we managed to register the team with the Youth Kitted League. We received the fixture list, and the team was down to play teams like LA Huskers, Norwich Devils, Nottingham Hoods and Glasgow Lions.

Their first game was on 26 July against the Devils at Norwich, where the Mavericks fielded only twenty players, so they knew they had an uphill task on their hands. The Devils won the toss and on their first drive they fumbled the ball, which the Mavericks recovered. Unfortunately the Mavericks' quarterback threw an interception and Norwich returned it for the first points of the game and added the two extra points, making the score 0–8 at the end of the first quarter. The second quarter belonged exclusively to the Devils, as they added two more touchdowns with the extra points being kicked, pushing the score at half-time to 0–22. In the second half, the Mavericks put in a superb effort by holding Norwich, recovering a fumble and an interception. Sadly the strain of playing both ways began to take its toll, and the Mavericks started to tire. Norwich took full advantage of the situation to score a further four touchdowns and added five extra points, making the final score 0–51.

Their next game was on 16 August against LA Huskers, to be played in Luton. After a start marred by mistakes, fumbles and interceptions, the Mavericks took the lead with a punt caught and returned for the score 6–0. The second quarter was scoreless, but the Mavericks were in firm control with Simon Booy and Jason Hall getting close to the goal line, so the score at the half remained at 6–0.

After the break, excellent running from Simon Booy and quarterback Scott Gallon added two further touchdowns and the two points after to raise the score to 20–0. The quarter ended in a flurry with the Huskers trying desperately to catch the rampant Mavericks. Eventually the Huskers' efforts were rewarded when their quarterback unleashed a fifty-two-yard bomb to their receiver in the end zone, and added the two points extra: 20–8. The final score of the game came from a one-yard rush from quarterback Scott Gallon, and with no point after the final score was 26–8.

Next, on 23 August it was the turn of the Nottingham Hoods in a game played in Derby, close to the Rolls-Royce factory. The Hoods won the toss and elected to receive. On their first drive they managed to get down to the Mavericks ten-yard line, but good defense denied them the touchdown. The action seesawed up and down the field and the quarter ended scoreless. The second quarter started in much the same way, but eventually the Hoods went over the line to open the scoring with no extra points. A second touchdown was called back because of a penalty in the backfield, so the score remained 0–6 at the half.

After the break, the Hoods stepped up the pressure and managed to score again, including the two points, to increase the tally to 0–14. After a second touchdown was called back for a penalty, it was now the turn of the Mavericks. The ball was on the Hoods three-yard line, the ball was snapped and handed off, the player was then tackled in the end zone for a two-point safety: 2–14. In the final period, the Mavericks held the Hoods until the last two minutes, then they [the Hoods] threw a pass to make the final score 2–20.

13 September saw the return match against the Huskers, this time at home, playing at Greenleys Rugby Club. On their second drive the Mavericks scored a touchdown with Mark Fitzgerald 6–0 and moved further ahead when Simon Booy rushed ten yards to score, plus the two points: 14–0. Russ Witton and Robin Cooper added two more touchdowns in the second quarter, making the

score at half-time 26–0. Russ Witton added his second touchdown in a scrappy third quarter, and Simon Booy rushed in for the two extra points: 34–0. The Huskers reduced the deficit with a two-point safety but the Mavericks finished well-deserved winners, at 34–2.

Now it was the return match against the Devils on 20 September, also at home. Much improved Mavericks held Norwich to within seconds of the end of the first half but fell foul to a fumble on the goal line, with Norwich going in to score with no point after: 0–6. The second half started with a supercharged Norwich taking control with a good drive down the field, only to be thwarted by the Mavericks' defense, with Russ Witton excelling himself. However, the Devils managed to add a further three touchdowns plus the points after to make the final score 0–27. The Mavericks played tough football and held Norwich to their lowest score all season.

For the final game of the regular season, it was the return match against the Hoods at home. The Mavericks won the toss and elected to receive. On their first drive they were pushed back to their own two-yard line. On the next play, the Hoods forced the offense back into the end zone for a two-point safety: 0–2. In the second quarter, the Mavericks' offense moved up a gear and, following a drive to the Hoods' five-yard line, new quarterback Mark Blancy completed a seven-yard pass to Matt Timms in the end zone: 6–2.

The second half then became an epic battle of defensive football played in oceans of mud. Exceptional work came from Jason Hall, Rob Cooper and Stuart Weaver, but the score remained 6–2.

The season's results gave the Mavericks a wild card chance in the play-offs, and they were drawn against the Glasgow Lions, who had home field advantage. This meant a very long and tiring journey to Glasgow. On their first play, the Mavericks lost the ball after a fumble on the line of scrimmage. Glasgow took advantage of the mistake and scored with a two-yard rush, and the point after attempt was good: 0–7. The Mavericks seemed unable to move the ball and the Lions scored two more touchdowns plus four extra points for 0–23. Towards the end of the first quarter the Mavericks gained a consolation score of six points from a seven-yard pass by Mark Blaney to Matt Timms in the end zone: 6–23. In the second quarter, the Lions took complete control adding a further twenty-one points with a seventy-seven-yard rush, a seven-yard rush and a twenty-two-yard pass, plus a one point and a two-point conversion, making the score 6–44 at the half.

The third and fourth quarters highlighted the experience of the Lions, with them appearing to score at will, with twenty-five points in the third and twenty points in the fourth, making a final score of 6–89. However, the lads had nothing to be ashamed of, in this their first season of competitive football.

It was time once again for the annual general meeting, which once again was very poorly attended. Luckily we had sufficient people to legally carry the vote, and Trina had returned to the fold and was elected Chairman once again. Bob Luddington had resigned his position as President and we decided that we would not elect anyone else to the position.

Once again it was time to sign up a new Head Coach, and the gentleman this time was Mr Hugh Fuller. He came to us with excellent credentials, and also introduced two new players, Warrick Mongston and his brother Nick. Warrick was also coach for the defensive backs, and we now looked forward with confidence to a more successful season.

The annual Dinner Dance went ahead very successfully, being held once more at the Woughton House Hotel, and this year the Clubman of the Year award was won by Neil Walton for his contribution to the club.

# *1993*

Things appeared to be settling down as we were still in the NDMA Coca-Cola League. We discovered our new coach was a very flamboyant character, turning up on game days with a rolled umbrella and wearing spats, but he nevertheless proved his worth.

We began with a couple of preseason games against Rockingham Rebels and Oxford Saints respectively. These games were played at a school on a pitch that was only seventy yards long, so the results would not have been recognised by the league. This was because our usual venue was unavailable due to rugby matches still being played. Our first meeting was with the Rockingham Rebels. The Rebels won the toss and elected to receive. On their first play, a superbly executed pass took the Pioneers by surprise, and resulted in a fifty-yard touchdown plus the two-point conversion: 0–8. The Pioneers followed this with a touchdown of their own also adding the two points to even the scores at 8–8. It was the Rebels who added a further eight points to take the lead at 8–16. The Pioneers replied with another touchdown but failed to add the point after: 14–16. Then just before the end of the half the Pioneers went ahead by a touchdown, making it 20–16 at the half.

In the second half, the Pioneers began to dominate the game and added a further twenty-eight unanswered points, with Lol Baker kicking the points after, making it 48–16, which was the final score.

Our next preseason was against the Oxford Saints and the Pioneers found themselves seven points down early in the first quarter: 0–7 There was no further score until in the second quarter the Pioneers drove downfield to the Saints two-yard line from where Nick Mongston ran in for the touchdown and Lol Baker kicked the extra point: 7–7. After being stopped on the twenty-yard line, the Saints went for a thirty-yard field goal and successfully put three more points on the board: 7–10. Late in the period, Nick again ran in for a six-yard touchdown, and Gladstone McKenzie converted for the two points, making the half-time score 15–10.

The third quarter saw some great pressure from Errol McCammon, which led to a touchdown by Paul Herbert, with Adrian Greaves adding the two points for 23–10. In spite of intense pressure from the Pioneers' defense, the Saints managed to run in a four-yard touchdown and kicked the point after: 23–17. The Pioneers now proceeded to dominate the rest of the game with a further three touchdowns from Gladstone McKenzie and one from our new signing, Ron Thomas. Points after came from Paul Herbert and Gladstone McKenzie making the final score 51–17.

Our regular season adversaries were West London Aces, Thames Valley Chargers, Cardiff Mets, Brighton B52s, Northants Storm and Glasgow Lions.

For the first game we travelled to Feltham in West London to take on the Aces, and it poured with rain all afternoon. This didn't worry the Pioneers, as they revelled in playing in the rain. The Pioneers kicked off but both teams were forced to punt. The Pioneers then drove down to the seven-yard line from where quarterback Paul Herbert ran six yards to set up a one-yard rush by Adrian Greaves for the score; the two-point attempt was no good: 6–0. The second quarter became a huge defensive battle with neither team being able to score.

There was no score in the third quarter either, but in the last period, the Aces finally broke through the Pioneer defense to level the score at 6–6. Then, in the dying seconds, the Aces completed a twenty-five-yard run to secure the victory at 6–12.

We now faced the Aces again with revenge in mind. Following the previous week's close defeat, the Pioneers came out looking tough. The Pioneers were driven downfield and the Aces capitalised with a touchdown but no point after: 0–6. Scott Gallon (recently promoted from the Mavericks), in his first season of senior football, was starting quarterback, he tried to put a good drive together but the Aces put paid to it with an interception. The Pioneers' defense held strong denying West London any advantage. The second quarter started with an Aces fumble recovered by Nick Tilbury, then the Aces gave up an interception, which John Stevenson snatched out of the air. The following play resulted in a touchdown for the Pioneers with a four-yards run by Nick Mongston: 6–6. The Pioneers were beginning to show their potential, especially on defense, where Nick Tilbury intercepted an Aces pass, and Scott finished it off with a brilliant twenty-three-yard pass to Robin Smart, who high stepped into the end zone, making the half-time score 12–6.

The third quarter started well for the Pioneers, with Tom Cregg recovering a fumble, and Nick Mongston completing a touchdown from five yards out: 18–6. The Pioneers' defense took over as West London tried in vain to break through. First Danny McAnuff intercepted, then Chris Carson recovered a punt, and Danny McAnuff intercepted deep in London territory. The offense could not match the defense, and with time ticking away the Aces came back. Behind a huge passing effort they scored another touchdown and threatened to tie the game. A monstrous effort from the home defense ensured there was no further score. Final score: 18–12.

For the next game we travelled to Maidenhead to take on the Thames Valley Chargers. On a beautiful summers day we had to face our biggest challenge yet as the Chargers were unbeaten in the conference.

The Pioneers won the toss and elected to receive but failed to move the ball. TVC then drove downfield and scored from a thirty-yard pass down the middle, and the kick for the point after was good: 0–7. There was no further score in the quarter.

TVC started the second quarter with a twenty-nine-yard field goal and continued to gain momentum, when a Pioneer punt was returned in a crazy play (we didn't know the rules that when receiving a punt, if the ball is touched and left to bounce it becomes a live ball and can be picked up by the opposition and run in for a touchdown) that resulted in six points plus a two-point conversion making the score 0–18 at half-time.

After the break, the Pioneers fumbled a punt, which the Chargers recovered in the end zone for six points, no point after. On a later TVC drive, they scored again from a ten-yard run, again with no point after, raising the score at the end of the third quarter 0–30. The final period saw some excellent defensive play by the Pioneers, but with time running out TVC scored once more from a ten-yard run to make the final score 0–36.

The following weekend we were on the road again to take on Cardiff. The game proved to be a tonic after the previous week's defeat as we won by a handsome margin.

The Pioneers kicked off and held Cardiff on their first drive. They moved the ball well and Steve Donegal scored a crushing twenty-yard running touchdown but failed with the extra point: 6–0. Starting quarterback Scott Gallon, despite a gallant effort, could not add to the score in the first quarter. The second quarter saw Steve Donegal again score with a twenty-three-yard run across the field into the end zone. With the score at 12–0, Cardiff came to life and scored with an excellent run back, plus the point after 12–7. The Pioneers replied with quarterback Scott Gallon rushing for an amazing sixty-four yards, but the offense couldn't finish the job!

After a tough talking-to, the Pioneers stepped up a gear when quarterback Paul Herbert, replacing an injured Scott Gallon, ran in for a three-yard touchdown after good work from Steve Donegal. The first half finished 18–7 to the dominant Pioneers.

The second half started with Danny McAnuff, now on defense, returning the kick-off to the one-yard line from where Ronnie Thomas finished the move to take it over the line for the touchdown, and the two-point conversion was added by Paul Herbert: 26–7. More scores were on the way with a fifty-nine-yard pass to Paul Skelly and a twenty-four-yard pass to Carl Appleton, raising the score to 42–7. Cardiff started a mini revival in the last period, with a touchdown but no point after for 42–13. However, the Pioneers pulled in a brace of interceptions by Steve Richards, which led to two more scores by Errol McCammon and James Douglas, making the score 56–13. Cardiff scored a late consolation touchdown and included a two-point conversion, but the Pioneers finished with a well-deserved 56–21 win.

Then once again we were up against the Thames Valley Chargers, this time on our home ground and we hoped that it would make a difference; time would tell.

The Chargers kicked off and the Pioneers were unable to

move the ball, but the defense held the Chargers, forcing them to punt. The Pioneers' following drive ended with the Chargers recovering a fumble on the two-yard line. The Pioneers' defense held for three downs but the Chargers scored on the fourth; the point after was unsuccessful, making the score 0–6. The first quarter saw no further score.

The second quarter saw the Chargers on the Pioneers' four-yard line. The attempted pass was intercepted in the end zone. There followed a spirited battle and Thames Valley finally added a further touchdown. The point after kick was blocked and Mark Floy ran it back ninety-two yards for a two-point safety: 2–12.

The third quarter once again saw the Chargers add a further seven points. The Pioneers also added two more points with a quarterback sack by Chris Carson in the end zone to bring the score to 4–19.

The final quarter was a tremendous battle by both teams until in the dying minutes the Chargers managed to add another touchdown, making the final score 4–25.

Now it was our turn to meet with Brighton over the next two weeks, starting with the away leg. We arrived at Withdean Stadium and found that a player who had been ejected from their last game wished to play. We argued that according to the rules the player concerned should serve a one-match ban. We finally agreed to consult the league, and their ruling was that he could play pending their appeal.

Following the kick-off neither team was able to move the ball and it wasn't until their quarterback threw a pass to the three-yard line that Brighton was able to score with a run to the end zone. No point after, so 0–6 at the end of the first quarter.

The Pioneers were not moving the ball well at the start of the second quarter and Brighton took over, but an excellent interception was run back to the B52s' one-yard line, which set up a scoring chance. On third down and three yards to go, Gladstone McKenzie made an acrobatic jump over the line to even the score at 6–6. The Pioneers' defense started to dominate, forcing Brighton to make mistakes, but the Pioneers were unable to click offensively, until Paul Herbert launched a massive punt to the B52s' one-yard line. Brighton escaped with a thirty-four-yard scramble upfield, but good work from the Pioneers got the ball back, and they finished the drive with a twenty-two-yard pass into the end zone, finishing the half 12–6 in the lead.

The second half began disastrously when the Pioneers fumbled after an eleven-yard return from the kick-off, giving Brighton good field position and presenting them with the chance to level the score at 12–12. The Pioneers' offense barely moved the ball, but good defense kept Brighton at bay, with a quarterback sack and two quarterback presses. Eventually Brighton broke through with a run of forty yards and a kicked point after: 12–19.

The fourth period opened with both teams punting, until the Pioneers were forced down to their one-yard line. The defense held out for three downs, but were penalised on the fourth, giving Brighton another four attempts. They scored on the next play: 12–25. They scored once more by running in an interception: 12–31. The kick for the extra point was blocked, and Danny McAnuff ran back eighty-four yards for a two-point safety, ending the game with a 14–31 scoreline.

Brighton came to town already in the play-offs, and were determined to make life hard for the Pioneers. It all began with both teams punting, and then the Pioneers' Matt Crone intercepted a pass and returned the ball twenty-five yards. A fumble then gave the ball back to Brighton, who drove down to the four-yard line and completed the drive with a touchdown plus the kicked extra point: 0–7.

The second quarter was again a stupendous defensive battle. Brighton intercepted the ball and made a brilliant run downfield but were unable to capitalise on the move. Things looked black for the Pioneers when their only quarterback, Scott Gallon, was injured and carried off the field. Former Northants junior receiver, Robin Smart, took over, and with two magnificent passes moved the team sixty yards downfield to the six-yard line. From there Robin Smart held on and took the ball in himself for six points. The two-point extra attempt was a spectacular catch by Carl Appleton in the end zone, for the Pioneers to take the lead 8–7.

The third and fourth quarters belonged to the defense, with Brighton having real trouble snapping the ball, and Milton

Keynes unable to maintain offensive pressure. Brighton's quarterback was sacked three times, then Brighton attempted a field goal, which was charged down, denying them any chance of adding to their score. The Pioneers punted to the fifty-yard line, giving Brighton a lot to do. With just over a minute left, Brighton made a crucial fourth and inches only to be pulled back twenty yards by penalties, and the game finished with the Brighton quarterback being sacked, making this the closest winning game for the Pioneers: 8–7.

We were very disappointed, as we never got the chance to play Cardiff at home, because they failed to turn up, so we were awarded the win 1–0 by default.

Having achieved the play-offs with a wild card position, we were drawn against the Glasgow Lions, which meant a long and tiring journey up the M6. Some of the team drove up on the Saturday, leaving the rest of us to set out early Sunday morning. One of the lads drove my car, carrying the equipment, and I drove a hired minibus with the remainder of the personnel.

The vehicle I was driving was not in the best condition, and seemed to balk at climbing hills, which added extra time to the journey; it took seven hours, to be exact.

With no quarterback, a severe depletion of players, plus the tiring journey to Glasgow, the Pioneers had the odds stacked against them. Indeed the odds proved too much, as Glasgow, 1993's top ranked team, crushed the Pioneers with a powerful first half passing display. Warrick Mongston took over as quarterback and with a restricted game plan, due to lack of players, mistakes were inevitable. Glasgow took an early lead, due in part to these mistakes. The Lions scored three quick touchdowns, but when our stand-in punter, Steve Donegal, kicked a huge fifty-six-yard punt the Pioneers thought their luck might be changing. The Lions started on their own twenty-yard line and with four passes they once again scored, to add to the Pioneers' misery. Glasgow intercepted a rare Mongston pass and were once more in control. The Pioneers had more headaches to come when veteran centre Dave (Basher) Watson was taken to hospital with a leg injury. Luckily it proved less serious than at first thought. Glasgow finished the half with two quick touchdowns to make the score 0–42.

The second half belonged to the Pioneers, who as always refused to lie down. The defense started holding the Scots, and Warrick finally made a breakthrough, handing off to Errol McCammon who ran forty yards to Glasgow's six-yard line. Two further plays moved the ball to the two-yard line from where Steve Donegal powered over goal line for the touchdown. Going for the two points, Carl Appleton received the catch in the end zone making the score 8–42. Glasgow in return drove the Pioneers to their one-yard line, but with a splendid show of defense the Scots were denied any further score.

The only plus on the day was that, according to league rules, the home team were obliged to pay us £200 towards our expenses. At the end of the season, we had managed a record of four wins and six losses, which was a vast improvement on last season.

As the Pioneers had failed to achieve any advancement beyond the play-offs, they arranged a to play an inter-conference match against the Northants Storm, who had some international players in their ranks, and came to Milton Keynes confident of victory. The Pioneers also had an international class player in Nigel Fleming, from the National and European Champions team, the London Olympians.

In the first quarter, scores were made by both teams with Paul Skelly doing the honours for the Pioneers, then with fumbles and punts the first quarter ended 6–6. The Pioneers started the second quarter with new quarterback Pete Underwood (a former junior national) and he was intercepted trying to fake a field goal. The Storm struggled on the ground, so their quarterback took to the air again and Francis Aliefeh intercepted the pass and obliged with his second touchdown from forty yards. After that, Nigel Fleming showed his talents with successive runs upfield to finish a trick pass from Pete Underwood for an easy two-yard score, finishing the half 12–12.

The second half started with Northants storming forward to no avail. They had a touchdown called back with penalties, and after that the Pioneers held firm. Somehow Northants lost control and the game swung the Pioneers' way, with many Storm players being penalised for abuse. Finally they realised their mistakes and the game ended effectively when the Storm scored again, despite their quarterback being sacked by Tom Cregg and Wayne Eaton. Time ticked by, and with the score at 12–20 the Pioneers tried in vain to recover after putting up a superb performance.

It was somewhere about now that the England team were going to play a game against the French in Dunkirk. I made enquiries among our supporters to see if anyone would like to go. A company in Birmingham were doing the trip by coach for £34, which included the cost of the ferry and admission to the stadium. I said I would hire a minibus and all I would charge was £20 per head inclusive of everything. As luck would have it, because of the Zeebrugge disaster, the ferry charge was only £8 each and included a courtesy bus to, and entry into, the stadium.

Everything went according to plan, and all had a great time. With regard to the game, I must admit that my recollection is very hazy, but if I remember rightly England won, but I cannot for the life of me remember the score. However, when it came time to leave for the ferry, everybody was still in the bar, so we decided to catch the later ferry at 10.30 p.m. This change meant that we arrived in Ramsgate in the early hours. Having finally got everyone on board the minibus, I had to drive into Sandwich to top up with petrol. On the journey home, I told the person sitting next to me, my stepdaughter, to make sure that I didn't doze off. Imagine my horror when I suddenly came too doing 60 mph on the hard shoulder of the M1! This experience made sure that I stayed wide awake for the rest of the journey, and luckily nobody had noticed my indiscretion.

By the time we reached Milton Keynes it was around 5 a.m., and after having finally delivered everyone to their own addresses, I arrived home at about seven o'clock, making it the end of a very long day. However, the main point of this story is that after deducting all the costs, i.e. the hire of the minibus, petrol and ferry fares, I still managed to put £80 into club funds, which gave me a feeling of great satisfaction.

This year was to see the last of the American Bowl games at Wembley Stadium, for reasons best known to the NFL. This time we were treated to a game between the Cowboys and the Lions. The attendance was the lowest of all the games at a modest

43,522. The game itself was cracker and resulted in a draw: 13–13.

As stated earlier we were playing at the rugby club's ground at Greenleys. They had decided to put on a fun day for their supporters and friends, and as we were guests we were invited to take part. As we wanted to do something different we suggested that we play a game against the rugby team. The idea was that the first half would be rugby and the second half American football without pads. The lads who were in attendance entered into the spirit of the idea and a great time was had by all. The result was a roaring success, and luckily it ended in a draw. Also on the lighter side we were invited to take part in another event that was in aid of a young girl suffering from cancer. Of course, we were only too pleased to oblige, and we put teams in for the tug of war and five-a-side football. We won the tug of war and received a very fine trophy for our contribution. In the five-a-side football we didn't do quite so well, but all in all it was a very successful afternoon's entertainment. I'm afraid I cannot recall how much money was raised, but I think it made everyone's efforts worthwhile.

Another incident during this season occurred at one of our home matches. As the weather was very pleasant and warm, I arranged for a local ice cream vendor to leave a mobile trailer for us to sell ice cream on a sale or return basis, and we would keep 35% of the takings. Everything was fine during the match, and the two cheerleaders who manned the trailer did very well. However, when everyone had gone home, I went to check on the field and found that the trailer had been left out in the open, instead of being moved back to the clubhouse, and it was probably local children who had stolen all of the remaining ice cream. The two people who were responsible for clearing the field I found drinking beer in the clubhouse. I must admit that I blew my top and gave them both a right dressing-down, as I had to pay for the stolen ice cream out of my own pocket, to the tune of £215. This just proved to me that if you want anything done it's best to do it yourself.

This was also the year that I retired from work, and on the day I retired I had to go and see the chairman of the company. I told him that I was retiring and he was surprised and asked how long I had been with the company. I told that I had served fifteen years and he said that the company would do something to mark the occasion. I told him that I knew exactly what the company could do for me and that was to give me £200, as I wanted to purchase a small public address system. He said that he meant something more personal, so I said that as I was heavily involved with the team then it was indeed very personal… Needless to say, I'm still waiting! He also said that if I had given as much dedication to my job as I had given to the team, then I would have been works' foreman. I laughed and reminded him in no uncertain manner that it was not company policy to promote within the company, so he was talking rubbish. Having retired, it meant that apart from anything else I could give my undivided attention to the team.

Margaret and I decided that we would have a holiday and agreed to take up an invitation to visit the USA. The invitation was from the parents of Jon Carter who was quarterback for the team back in 1990, and we went off to spend three weeks with his family who lived near Pittsburgh. When we arrived at Pittsburg Airport, Jon Sr and Pat were there to meet us. As we passed through customs we turned to go through the door and there they were holding up a big placard saying, 'Welcome to the USA, Margaret and Ernie'. We then had to stand there holding the placard while Jon videoed us. We collected our luggage and made our way to Jon's car, and we were then driven straight to a hotel for a meal. We then were driven to the family home in Claysville. The holiday was fantastic, as our hosts were generous to a fault, and the first thing that Jon Sr did was to give me a card, like a credit card, which allowed us to stay at certain hotels on a two-for-one basis. This came in very handy, as on the first weekend they took us to Washington DC, where we stayed at the Hilton Hotel in Gaithersburg, then spent the following day in Washington visiting some of the museums. Jon Sr and I went to the Aerospace Museum, where I tried to educate Jon about the various aircraft, as this had been a passion since I was a boy. I also pointed out the doodlebug that they had on display, and told him about some of my experiences with the flying bombs during World War II. Meanwhile Margaret and Pat visited another of the museums in the area, which dealt with the dresses of the country's leading women. We then travelled through the Gettysburg battlefields, where Pat pointed out her uncle's name on the huge memorial, and on up to Amish country where we stayed at a small motel, finally making our way back to Claysville and the farm. Then, on the second weekend they held a picnic at their house for us to meet all of their friends and relatives. It was a little bit embarrassing meeting all these people, but I must admit they were all very friendly, which did allay some of our initial misgivings, and they were fascinated by our British accents.

Jon Sr took a day off work to take Margaret and me to the American Football Hall of Fame in Canton, Ohio. This was a fantastic experience, and we were very surprised at the size of the building inside, as from the outside it didn't look all that big. The way it was laid out was fascinating and it gave us an insight into the origins of the sport, such as that the game originated in Pennsylvania in 1892, and the original uniform was comprised of a jersey and knee-length trousers and the helmet was leather; they also wore a patch of leather covering their nose. We spent quite a long time walking around looking at the fascinating exhibits and absorbing the unique atmosphere.

On the final weekend they took us to Niagara Falls. After visiting the falls from the American side we discovered that there was no accommodation available in Niagara, so we went over the border into Canada and on to Toronto, where we stayed at two different hotels, because it appeared that the hotels were full due to conferences. When we arrived back in Niagara we hunted around for somewhere to park, and finally ended up on the outskirts of the town. The cost to park was $8, which I thought was a bit steep until, when we got to the place we had to pay, we were given stickers to use on an articulated tram that they called a 'people-mover'. It was propelled by propane gas, and the sticker entitled us to get on and off the bus as many times as we liked. All in all, it was an unforgettable experience.

Another outing they took us on was a visit to Ladbrookes to watch some trotting races. Jon Sr kept on trying to persuade me to place a bet on one of the races. I repeatedly told him that I was not a gambling man, but he insisted. I finally gave in and on consulting the race card, I noticed that in race five there was a horse running called 'Better than Sex'. I said, 'Right that's the one,' and got Margaret to put $6 on to win.

Jon tried to persuade me to back it each way, but I said, 'No, it either wins or it doesn't.' Happily it did win, but Margaret had taken two of my six dollars and put them on another horse, which was still running!

Back in England, the annual general meeting once again saw some changes of personnel. Robert Wade, an ex-player, was elected as Chairman, Dave Lane as Secretary, and I was elected to a new post of General Manager. We also incorporated Gwen Kiely as Coordinator for the cheerleaders. Trina Collins had given in her resignation, as she felt that she could not give enough of her attention to the club.

The annual Dinner Dance was again held at the Woughton House Hotel and as usual we gave every player a trophy. The coaches were asked to vote for the players who were to receive the special trophies, i.e. Best Offense, Best Defense and Most Promising Rookie. The winner for the Clubman of the Year award this year was Tony Reed, a man whose dedicated attitude was a great asset to the club, and the award was richly deserved.

# 1994

We weren't to know it at the time, but this was to be our finest year to date, as you will see. We signed up two new coaches for the coming season, John Parker and Allan Brown. These two men had had extensive playing experience with the top clubs, and as I said, it proved to be a sound move. We also imported an American quarterback by the name of James Madison. He proved to be a great asset to the team. I don't believe that I have mentioned before our commitment to Americans as laid down by the league. If we imported a player from America then we were obliged to pay his return airfare, find him accommodation, and pay him £100 per week. With Jimmy we rented a two-bedroom house, which was very close to where I live, and we also put another American player in with him, named Chris Dahl, who incidentally had been living with us, and he also had his girlfriend with him. It worked very well, and Jimmy was always ready to help out if he was needed, like when we had to mow the grass on the field before we could play any games.

This was the year that British American Football finally got its act together, with the remaining two leagues merging to come under the British American Football Association (BAFA), as the British Senior League, so at last the sport gained some sort of credibility, and was finally recognised by the Sports Council as an official sport. It was hoped that the new set-up would perhaps encourage more sponsorship from the business world and more coverage from the media.

It seems that our reputation was being noticed around the league as we began to attract some very experienced players from far and wide. As I mentioned earlier, among the costs to the players was supplying photographs for registration cards. It seemed that the price of using the machines kept on increasing, so to help out I took my camera to training sessions and set it up nine feet from a wall, then asked the player to stand against the wall and not move. I then took two pictures, which when developed and cut down were the correct size for passports. This was just one of the ways we tried to save the players extra expense; I will explain further later on.

We began with a preseason game against the Southern Seminoles, which we played in Basingstoke. The match was played on Astroturf, which was kept well watered, as we found out at halftime. The pitch was surrounded by a high wire fence and at the break they turned on the sprinklers, and quite a few of us got rather wet, as we were some way away from the only gate.

There was no score in the first quarter, as both teams fought for supremacy. It was after the change of ends that Basingstoke drove downfield and scored a field goal from the twenty-nine-yard line to go three points up at the half. After the break, the Pioneers broke through their defense, for Steve Donegal to race sixty-six yards for the touchdown, with no point after 6–3. The fourth quarter saw some good defensive plays, but the Seminoles finally broke through to score from thirty-nine yards and add the extra point: 6–10. The Pioneers were on their own two-yard line and were caught in the end zone for a two-point safety, making the final score 6–12.

We began the season proper with a home game against the London Rockets, a team with a reputation for tricks and fast players. Such opponents did not overawe the Pioneers, as we felt that we, too, could come up with a few tricks of our own. This game introduced our new American quarterback, James Madison, who, with a little help, was going to prove that the Pioneers were the ones to beat.

The first half was a dour battle, with the Rockets scoring two touchdowns – twelve points – and the Pioneers one touchdown and two points making the half-time score 8–12. The Rockets added a further six points 8–18, before the Pioneers retaliated with a touchdown from a thirty-one-yard pass to Carl Appleton and Gladstone McKenzie adding the two points: 16–18. London again punished the Pioneers with a completion and two points to create a ten-point difference at 16–26. With time running out, the Pioneers hurried along the offense with a hard fought drive starring Clive Etienne, leaving Gladstone McKenzie to score on a three-yard run, and American Chris Dahl with the extra two points to make the final score 24–26.

Next we once again met our old rivals the Brighton B52s, on our home ground. In the first quarter, a Brighton pass was intercepted by John Stevenson and returned twenty yards for the touchdown, no extra points: 6–0. There was no further scoring during the rest of the quarter, despite some valiant attempts by both sides. The second period produced another touchdown for the Pioneers when Robin Smart caught a thirty-three-yard pass to score and Gladstone McKenzie added the two points extra as he fought his way into the end zone: 14–0. Brighton replied following a good drive with a four-yard run to bring the half-time score to 14–6.

The second half produced some more exciting football, and during the third quarter Brighton scored their second touchdown, again the two-point attempt was no good: 14–12. In the last period, the Pioneers were only able to add two more points with a safety to make the final score 16–12.

Then came our first away game, and we travelled to Ipswich to play the Cardinals. From the start the Pioneers showed determination, and early in the game, following a twenty-eight-yard run by Gladstone McKenzie, they put the first points on the board: 6–0. Then later in the same quarter, Chris Dahl completed a drive with a five-yard run to raise the score to 12–0. In the second period, Ipswich rallied and scored with a thirty-seven-yard reception and added the point after: 12–7. This was how the half finished.

The third quarter was scoreless as both defenses held firm and it wasn't until the fourth quarter that the Pioneers were able to drive down to the one-yard line from where James Madison, the quarterback, went over the line with a quarterback sneak. The point after attempt was unsuccessful. In the dying seconds of the game the Pioneers recovered the ball with an interception and ran out the clock, making the final score 18–7.

Again we were on the move, this time to Tiptree to take on the Titans. The Pioneers opened the scoring with Clive Etienne returning a ninety-yard punt and Nick Tilbury making a catch in the end zone for two points: 8–0. There was no more scoring until late in the second quarter when the Clive Etienne completed a fifteen-yard reception for the touchdown, and our newly signed running back, Ryan Holness, caught the ball for the extra two points: 16–0.

Following the break the Titans retaliated with a drive to the Pioneers nine-yard line, and completed the move with a catch in the end zone. They elected to kick for the extra point, and were successful making the score 16–7. The final quarter saw both teams moving the ball up and down the pitch to no avail, so the score remained at 16–7.

It was prior to one of our home games that I once again injured myself. After each game, we would dismantle the goalposts and store them at the farm belonging to Derek Austin, Margaret's boss. On this particular day I had driven down to the farm with several of the lads to collect the goalposts, for which Derek loaned us his pick up truck. The posts had been stored in a disused lorry in one of the barns, and I went in to make sure that we could easily move them. The sides of the lorry had been returned to the closed position, so I climbed onto the rear wheel and grabbed the side panel. Unfortunately the panel had not been secured and I fell flat on my back. The steel panel hit both of my ankles and I thought that I had broken them. After yelling at the top of my voice I was finally rescued and hobbled outside, where Derek's wife, Terry, came over with a bag of frozen peas to try and stop the swelling. When I went back and looked at where I had fallen I realised that I had been very lucky, as right beside where I fell was a spiked farming implement.

For the next match, which was the first of two inter-conference games, the Plymouth Admirals had to travel to us at our home ground at Greenleys. The Admirals at this point were at the top of their conference, and the match turned into a test of strength and stamina as both teams fought for domination. The first quarter saw the Admirals open the scoring with a twenty-one-yard reception plus the point after: 0–7. The Pioneers replied immediately, with Clive Etienne also making a twenty-one-yard catch, but failed with the two-point attempt leaving Plymouth in the lead: 6–7. Once again Plymouth came back with a seven-yard catch and added the kicked extra point, making the score at the change of ends 6–14.

The second period turned into a defensive battle, and there was no further score before the end of the half.

There was only one score in the third quarter when the Pioneers produced a superb thirty-six-yard run up the middle by Gladstone McKenzie, and Clive Etienne added the two points with a catch levelling the score at 14–14.

The final period saw the Pioneers add two further scores, the first with a one-yard rush by Ryan Holness who also claimed the two extra points, and this was followed by another Clive Etienne seven-yard reception and the two extra points by Dean McBroom to raise score to 30–14. Plymouth, however, did not take it lying down, they scored a further two touchdowns with sixty-four-yard and forty-yard receptions respectively, but failed with the conversions, making the final score 30–26. This proved to be a very balanced and exciting game.

For our next game we travelled down to Bristol to play the Aztecs. This match was totally dominated by the Pioneers and they held Bristol to a whitewash.

It all began in the first quarter. The Aztecs were forced to punt, and the Pioneers took over on their own forty-five-yard line and drove down to the two-yard line from where Errol McCammon ran in for the touchdown and Robin Smart added the two points: 8–0. Later in the period, Chris Dahl set up a drive from an interception on the fifty-yard line. The following drive resulted in an eleven-yard catch by Clive Etienne in the end zone, and Adrian Greaves added the two points with a run: 16–0. There was one score in the second quarter following the Aztec's quarterback being sacked by Tom Cregg on the Pioneers' twenty-yard line. This set up a drive, which culminated in a fifteen-yard reception by Nick Tilbury with no extra points, making the score 22–0 at the half-time break.

The third quarter saw the Pioneers' defense in excellent form. Ryan Holness tipped a pass, which was caught by Graham Martin and returned twelve yards for the score, and the two points were added by Steve Donegal: 30–0.

In the final period, Carl Reeves caught his second interception to set up a drive, which resulted in a four-yard run by Steve Donegal for the touchdown. Chris Dahl gained the two points,

38–0. Then, with eight seconds left in the game, they set up for a field goal, but it was a fake and the quarterback James Madison passed the ball thirty yards to Clive Etienne, who broke two tackles to score, resulting in a final score of 44–0.

Incidentally, it was stated in their programme that they never expected to win, which in my view was very defeatist, and probably tended to demoralise their players. It was at this game that one of our players had to be taken to hospital, and as we were not allowed to play without an ambulance in attendance, the game was suspended until the ambulance returned, which was about three parts of an hour. Unfortunately, this situation occurred twice, which was very frustrating. Anyway, when our player returned it appeared that he was high on the medication the hospital had given him; luckily, his wife was there to drive him home.

With four games to go to the end of the regular season, the Pioneers played host to the Ipswich Cardinals in a match played in hot and sticky conditions. The first half was completely dominated by the Pioneers with four unanswered touchdowns plus three two-point and one one-point conversions as listed below.

The first score was in the opening quarter. After a sixty-five-yard drive to the seven-yard line, the running back Steve Donegal rushed the necessary yardage to score, and Errol McCammon ran in the extra two points: 8–0. In the second quarter, the Pioneers showed just how determined they were to go for the championship by adding the other three touchdowns. The first came from Robin Smart with a sixteen-yard reception, and Allan Brown added the two points: 16–0. The second came from a twenty-one-yard run again by Steve Donegal with Francis Aliefeh adding the two points: 24–0. To round off the quarter Clive Etienne made a fifteen-yard reception, and this time Dean McBroom kicked the point after: 31–0.

From the second half kick-off, Allan Brown made a fantastic seventy-seven-yard return, which set up Chris Dahl on the one-yard line. There followed a rush into the end zone for the touchdown but no point after: 37–0. At this point the Cardinals rallied at last to get themselves on the scoreboard: 37–6. The final period saw our James Madison move the offense on a seventy-yard drive, which he capped with a three-yard dive to raise the score by a further six points: 43–6. But Ipswich were not finished yet, and came back to score their second touchdown to make the final score 43–12.

The next game was a real needle match between the Pioneers and the London Rockets, and proved to be just that, as the Pioneers desperately needed to win to continue their quest for the championship. The game was played in brilliant sunshine at the Rockets' ground in Finsbury Park, and developed into the battle royal we had expected.

The Rockets were the first to score with no added points – 0–6 – and then the Pioneers took over the ball and on the ensuing drive were on fourth and ten. James Madison threw a twenty-six-yard reception to Clive Etienne for the touchdown. Ryan Holness ran in the two-point conversion: 8–6. Despite frenzied efforts, neither team could add to their scores, and the first quarter finished with a scoreline of 8–6 in the Pioneers' favour.

The second half began with the Pioneers receiving the ball, and Ryan Holness made a superb run down the side line, breaking five tackles, to complete thirty-two yards to add six more points plus two for the point after by Steve Donegal: 16–6. There was no more scoring in the third quarter, but the final period proved to be the most exciting of the match. The defensive battle continued to within eleven minutes of the final whistle. It was then that the Rockets scored their second touchdown, but no point after: 16–12. With 3 minutes 50 seconds to go, the Rockets scored again and added the extra point to take the lead: 16–19. With just 1 minute 20 seconds and three points' difference, James engineered a seventy-five-yard drive, and with eighteen seconds to go produced a trick play. James Madison took the snap and passed the ball back to Ryan Holness, who then threw a four-yard pass to Clive Etienne for the touchdown. The point after attempt was fumbled, but the Pioneers regained the lead: 22–19. The ensuing kick-off left the Rockets with forty-seven yards to go and one second left. The quarterback threw a completed pass, but the receiver was stopped on the one-yard line by Dean McBroom to guarantee the win for the Pioneers, and a place in the play-offs.

However, the match was not without incident as there was a controversy over the final play. The Rockets' Head Coach, Tyrone Lindsey, claimed that his player had crossed the line, and during the heated discussion that followed, Tyrone Lindsey was alleged to have struck one of the officials. The league's reaction to the incident was to ban Tyrone Lindsey from the sport for life. As the Rockets folded soon after, we were thinking of signing Tyrone as a coach, so I contacted the league to verify the situation. It transpired that the evidence was very sketchy and no firm action had been taken. In the meantime, Tyrone had decided to take a year off, so I will continue this saga later.

To return to the rest of the season, our next match was against our old rivals, Brighton B52s, on their home ground, and a win would guarantee our position as South East Conference Champions.

The game kicked off and the first quarter was scoreless as both teams fought to move the ball without much success. The start of the second quarter was a repeat of the first until Ryan Holness broke through with a four-yard run; he also added the two points to open the scoring at 8–0. However, on the ensuing kick-off Brighton caught the ball and returned it a stunning ninety-two yards for the touchdown. The extra point attempt was unsuccessful, making the score 8–6 at half-time.

The third period was again a defensive battle until in the last few minutes Clive Etienne completed a thirty-one-yard reception in the end zone to increase the score to 14–6. The final period saw the fired up Pioneers increase the pressure, and eventually they managed to break through when Errol McCammon broke two tackles to complete a twenty-one-yard run for the third touchdown but no point after. The final score was 20–6.

The final game of the regular season was played at Greenleys, between the Pioneers and the Tiptree Titans. The Titans had beaten the London Rockets quite handsomely the previous week, so they were all fired up and ready to do battle. However, the Pioneers were hell-bent on achieving the Championship, and nothing or no one was going to deny them.

The Pioneers won the toss and elected to receive, and on fourth down James Madison fired a forty-two-yard pass to Clive

Etienne to set up the Pioneers on the Titans' one-yard line. From there, Gladstone McKenzie powered over the line for the touchdown and Robin Smart added the two points with a catch: 8–0. There was no further scoring in the period. On the Pioneers' first play of the second quarter, Allan Brown scored with a forty-six-yard reception and another touchdown; he also completed the pass from Ryan Holness for the two points: 16–0.

The third quarter was an outstanding display of defensive football with neither team conceding a score. The fourth quarter again began with the defenses not allowing much movement of the ball until Ryan Holness, aided by some superb blocking, broke through for a forty-six-yard rushing touchdown, but no extra point: 22–0. Later, following a stupendous punt by Steve Donegal, Conroy Brown (Allan's brother) tackled the runner in the end zone for a two-point safety: 24–0. Near the end of the quarter, Dean McBroom made an interception, and on the following series James Madison threw a sixteen-yard pass to Ray Hunt who was brought down on the Titans' one-yard line. With first and goal, James Madison scored with a quarterback sneak, bringing the final score to 30–0. The win gives the Pioneers home field advantage throughout the play-offs.

The season was the finest in the Pioneers' history by going 9–1, and silencing a lot of our critics. Now we were geared up to take on the Plymouth Admirals again in the quarter-finals.

The game was played before the largest crowd we had had all season, and included a lot of very noisy supporters from Plymouth, who made sure that everyone knew they were there.

After the kick-off both teams were forced to punt, and it was on the Pioneers second possession that Errol McCammon broke through with a forty-three-yard run. In the same series, Clive Etienne made a ten-yard reception and then he made a further six-yard catch in the end zone: 6–0. The rest of the quarter was dominated by the defenses, ensuring that the scoreline remained unaltered right through the second period as well.

After the break, the Pioneers' defense continued to excel. Then when the offense took over, James Madison fired a twenty-three-yard pass to Allan Brown, who leapt above two defenders to snatch the ball; then on a subsequent play Allan Brown again caught a six-yard pass in the end zone to lift the score to 12–0. Into the fourth quarter, the Pioneers' defense gave an excellent performance and finally allowed the offense to run out the clock. 12–0 was the final score, and paved the way for the semi-final to be played against Brighton B52s, with the Pioneers meeting them for the third time this season.

As we had already beaten them twice before during the season, Brighton was definitely geared up to go for revenge. However, the Pioneers had other ideas, and stated their intention on their first possession with a fifty-eight-yard run by Steve Donegal but no point after: 6–0. With the Pioneers' defense on form there was no further score in the quarter. In the second quarter, Allan Brown capped a sixty-four-yard drive with a twenty-two-yard reception for the touchdown; Adrian Greaves added the two points: 14–0. The B52s' offense then drove downfield and completed a fourteen-yard reception on a fake field goal. The extra point was good: 14–7. On the ensuing kick-off, our Allan Brown ran the ball back ninety-two yards for the touchdown and Gladstone McKenzie added the two points: 22–7. This started a period of dominant football by the Pioneers, which was evident when Tom Cregg recovered a Brighton fumble deep in their own territory. On the ensuing play, Nick Tilbury made a twenty-six-yard reception to score, but no point after: 28–7. Brighton were forced to punt, and it was then the offensive line created a huge hole for Gladstone McKenzie to run seventy-six yards to pay dirt; Errol McCammon added the two points extra to make it 36–7 at the half.

In the opening moments of third quarter, Brighton rallied to complete a fifteen-yard run for their second touchdown and added the extra point: 36–14. Once again Allan Brown caught and returned the kick-off seventy-seven yards to increase the score to 42–14. On the first play of the final quarter the Pioneers ended another finely engineered drive by James Madison, with a thirty-one-yard reception by Robin Smart in the end zone, but no point after: 48–14. Following a drive by James Madison to the one-yard line, he completed the scoring with a quarterback sneak plus two points by Allan Brown, making the final score 56–14.

After the game I was talking to their management, who were

old friends, and they said, and I quote, 'The problem is that every time we meet to play, the Pioneers get better' – a very nice compliment. Now we were set to take on the Bedford Bombadiers in our first final. A win would see us promoted to Division 1, taking on the country's top teams.

This very important game was played in Leicester at Saffron Lane Stadium, and would mark a significant point in the evolution of the Pioneers.

The game began with the Pioneers electing to kick-off. The Bombadiers were forced to punt and the Pioneers were soon on the attack. They put together a good drive, but were unable to press home the advantage. Again Bedford were denied any yardage, and when the Pioneers regained possession, they marched down to the seventeen-yard line, where James Madison, in his last game before returning to the States, handed off to Steve Donegal, who dashed past the defense to open the scoring; the point after attempt was no good: 6–0. The second quarter started with the Pioneers on Bedford's nine-yard line, they moved the ball to the four-yard line, from where Adrian Greaves bulldozed into the end zone again with no extra points: 12–0. However, before the half was up Bedford managed to get back into the game with a touchdown of their own, making it 12–6.

The third quarter was scoreless and it wasn't until late in the final period that Steve Donegal broke through several tackles to scamper sixty-five yards to seal our victory: 18–6.

After several years of struggling to gain the recognition they deserved, the Pioneers, and our new cheerleaders, who had had only three weeks of training sessions, ended an exciting season by becoming Division 2 Champions in a tense confrontation. The crowd were magnificent cheering the team on throughout the game. We could now look forward to competing in Division 1 in 1995.

It was this year that our endeavours to obtain a ground of our own were realised. The council offered us a piece of ground at Denbigh North. It was part of a sporting complex, and the site allocated to us was about four acres, and once again I made a model of the proposed layout. Things were progressing well, with the signing of the papers imminent, when I received a telephone call out of the blue. There were plans afoot to build a stadium in the centre of Milton Keynes, but it was being built for the National Hockey Association. The telephone call I had was from the secretary of the Association offering us the opportunity to play in the stadium when it was completed. I reported back to the committee with the news, and after some discussion it was decided to accept the offer. I now had to go back to the council to explain why we were not taking up the offer of Denbigh North. The council were very understanding, when I explained that for us to develop Denbigh North would cost a lot of money, which we didn't have at the time, whereas if we played at the stadium all the development was done.

I managed to obtain plans of the stadium, courtesy of Mr Hildreth, a councillor, and had several meetings with both the Hockey Association and the contractors. The pitch was made of Astroturf and it worked out that we would only be able to get a ninety-yard pitch with ten-yard end zones, instead of the full 100 yards. This arrangement was satisfactory with the league, so I went ahead with plans to sink the bases for the goalposts. Imagine my horror when the Contractor said that it would cost £2,000 *per hole*, just to sink a tube 3.5 feet long by 3 inches in diameter to support the post! I blew my top and told them that I would do it myself, as all I needed to do was to dig a hole a foot square and 3.5 feet deep, then drop the tube in the hole and surround it with concrete, which is exactly what we did at Manor Fields and Greenleys.

As the stadium would not be finished until 1996, we left Greenleys, as there was talk that they would be moving, and we returned to Manor Fields, as it was now under new management.

I kept in touch with the stadium to ensure that we were notified of any changes that would affect us. Actually, quite a lot of changes were made to the original plans because of escalating costs. For instance, there would only be four changing rooms instead of eight, and several other cost-cutting exercises. In line with our aims of making this a family-orientated club, we supplied the players with chocolate bars at training, and on game days we made bread puddings and banana cake. The cost of these treats came out of Margaret's own purse, and it was greatly appreciated by all concerned. By this time the players had given Margaret the title of 'Lady M', which I feel showed the level of respect they held for her.

As I mentioned earlier, we had to say goodbye to James Madison, as he was only with us for the one season. However, he managed to stay long enough to attend our end of season Dinner Dance. This year it was organised by Dave Lane and his wife, Ann; they had booked the evening at the Trusthouse Forte hotel in Central Milton Keynes, and had also booked a hypnotist. This decision proved to be a bit controversial, but nevertheless it went down well. James Madison had been told that he would not have to bring a suit so he turned up on the night in shorts; he was a little upset, but because of his nature he was still the life and soul of the party. Before he left we gave him a T-shirt and a trophy as souvenirs, and I understand that when he got home, back in New York, he set up a shrine to the memory of the Pioneers, such was the effect we had on him.

At this stage the AGM's were fast becoming a farce as attendances continued to drop, and we tried a new approach to the way the administration was structured. What we did was to divide the administration into two categories. Firstly, there was a Management Executive of five people, namely myself as General Manager, Brian Day as Secretary, Margaret Gifford as Treasurer, Dave Lane as PR Manager and Dean McBroom as Player Rep. The Policy Committee consisted of five members, Eif Williams as team manager, Paul Harvey as Equipment Manager, Dave Watson as Alternative Player Rep, Sharon Benson as Cheerleader Rep and Tom Cregg as PR Assistant.

# 1995

We were very pleased that John Parker and Allan Brown agreed to stay on as our Head Coaches, which gave us a little of the continuity of training that we had been missing over the years.

We had stopped doing the attendances at school fêtes and such, as now the team comprised of players from all over Southern England, with very few from Milton Keynes, so it was difficult to get them all together for activities other than training and games, although a lot of training sessions were badly attended, much to the annoyance of the coaches. It was mainly because of the number of players who lived outside the Milton Keynes area that we had to try and help to alleviate some of the travel costs. This meant that we tried several different venues, mostly in Luton. Luton was easily accessible, being just off the M1, and catered well for the players who travelled from London. We approached the Luton rugby club, and they were very obliging, and we trained there for several weeks. It was during one of our training sessions that I was called on to the pitch to do some repairs to a player's helmet. I was busy trying to put right the problem when I was knocked flat on my face by one of the players executing a move. Having experienced the force of impact I now know why they wear all that padding! However, our liaison with the rugby club didn't last, as they had to do some renovations on their pitches.

It was then that we were introduced to the Vauxhall Leisure complex and were allowed to use a superb Astroturf pitch. By moving the training out of Milton Keynes we did begin to get better attendances at the sessions, and we all appreciated the facilities that the leisure centre offered.

For this season we signed up another American quarterback by the name of Chuck Lynch, who we hoped would help us as James Madison had done.

We were now in Division 1, and the opposition was pretty

formidable with teams like Storm-Bombadiers, (a merger between Northants and Bedford), Leicester Panthers, Leeds Cougars, London Olympians and Birmingham Bulls.

In the opening game the Pioneers took on the Storm-Bombadiers. Neither team was able to score in the first quarter, and it wasn't until the final two minutes of the half that the opposition broke through to open the scoring with seven points: 0–7.

After the break, the Pioneers were intent on getting their revenge. Ryan Holness opened the scoring for the Pioneers with an interception, which he returned thirteen yards, and Steve Donegal kicked the point after levelling the scores at 7–7. Then later in the quarter Steve Donegal scored again on a five-yard run, but failed to get the extra point: 13–7. In the fourth quarter, following a sixty-four-yard drive, Ryan Holness scored his second touchdown from six yards out, and the point after was added by Steve Donegal: 20–7. The Pioneers continued their rout with Clive Etienne catching a thirty-four-yard bomb from Chuck Lynch in the end zone for another score, with Steve Donegal again adding the point after: 27–7. However, the Pioneers were not finished yet, as in the dying seconds of the game, veteran Tom Cregg recovered a fumble in the end zone for the final score of 33–7.

The Pioneers paid their second visit to Leicester in an attempt to reverse the result of the preseason game played in April. They arrived at Saffron Lane with a bigger squad than before after signing several new experienced players, who would be an undoubted asset in their attempt for play-off contention.

The first half produced two quarters of two well-balanced defenses neither of which allowed the other to break the deadlock, and it wasn't until the third quarter that Leicester managed to open the scoring with a fifty-two-yard reception; the two-point conversion was unsuccessful: 0–6. There was no further scoring until the commencement of a mad fourth quarter. The Panthers capped an eighty-five-yard drive with a twelve-yard reception to bring the score to 0–12. On the next play, Chuck Lynch rolled out of the pocket and completed a forty-nine-yard pass to Clive Etienne in the end zone. Steve Donegal kicked the extra point, putting the Pioneers on the scoreboard: 7–12. The Panthers then drove downfield, aided by some very dubious penalties, ending in a one-yard run for the touchdown, followed by the two-point conversion: 7–20. But the Pioneers were not finished yet, and on their next drive Steve eluded the left tackle to complete an eleven-yard run, the point after kick was tipped and hit the post: 13–20. On the Panthers' next drive the Pioneers forced a fumble and recovered the ball with 1 minute 11 seconds left in the game. After a couple of short gains, Chuck was forced to throw a 'Hail Mary' which was unsuccessful. Final score: 13–20.

For the following match, the Pioneers were at home to Leeds Cougars in this the third game of the season. After their defeat the previous week the Pioneers were determined to go all out to win.

The Pioneers kicked off and held the Cougars to negative yardage, then the Pioneers took over the ball and Ryan Holness capped a fifty-eight-yard drive with a three-yard run to score and the extra point was added by Steve Donegal: 7–0. Later in the quarter, Ryan Holness recovered a fumble, then Chuck Lynch connected with Steve Sobers with a thirty-yard pass to score, but no point after: 13–0. In the second quarter, the Cougars, who were fielding only eighteen players, showed their mettle by denying the Pioneers any further score.

After the break, the Pioneers stepped up the pressure, and following a sixty-six-yard drive, which included a thirty-six-yard bomb to Steve Sobers, Steve Donegal went over the left tackle for a three-yard run to pay dirt, and he also kicked the extra point: 20–0. In the last quarter, Ryan Holness was in the limelight again. He took the handoff from Chuck Lynch, and seeing a defensive wall ahead he turned and ran upfield, turned again and launched a pass to Steve Sobers, who then completed the fifty-three yards for a touchdown, and Steve Donegal once again kicked the ball for the extra point: 27–0. This was the final score, and Leeds are to be commended for their determination with the odds stacked against them.

We now had to face the Panthers again, in the return match we dearly wanted to win, but time would tell…

Milton Keynes received the ball on the opening kick-off and fumbled it. Leicester recovered it and needed only four plays to open an early 0–7 lead. The Pioneers were quick to respond when Ryan Holness broke numerous tackles for an eighty-one-yard touchdown run, which was the longest rushing touchdown in the history of the Pioneers, Steve Donegal added the extra point to level the scores at 7–7. Later in the period, Ryan Holness bagged an interception, which set up the offense for a thirty-one-yard field goal kicked by Steve Donegal to give the Pioneers a 10–7 lead. The lead changed hands again when the Pioneers fumbled the ball and the Panthers took it over the line with a quarterback keep: 10–13.

After the break, the Pioneers regained the lead by storming down the field to the one-yard line, from where Steve Donegal blasted into the end zone, adding the point after himself: 17–13. The defensive battle hotted up as the Pioneers struggled to hold on to their slender lead. Late in the period, Leicester managed to convert a crucial fourth down into a touchdown. The point after attempt was blocked for a 17–19 lead, which they were able to defend successfully to the final whistle.

It was now our turn to meet the London Olympians, who were also European Champions, but the Pioneers were not overawed, and put up a very spirited performance by holding them to a scoreless first quarter. In the second quarter, it was a fumble by the Pioneers that set London up to score; the attempted point after was blocked: 0–6. The Pioneers responded when Chuck Lynch capped a fifty-eight-yard drive with a thirty-eight-yard touchdown pass to Clive Etienne. Steve Donegal scored the extra point giving us the lead 7–6. But it was short-lived, as London scored again just before the end of the quarter to make it 7–12 at the half.

Following the break the Pioneers completely lost the plot with unforced errors, which cost them dearly, as London capitalised on the mistakes. In the Pioneers' defence, they did deny them the points after. The score was now 7–24. In the fourth quarter, the Olympians increased their lead to 7–31. To prove that they were not finished yet, Francis Aliefeh bagged an interception and weaved downfield for fifty-five yards to score, with Chuck making the two-point conversion for a final score of 15–31.

It was after this match that we were compelled to ask for the resignation of Chuck Lynch (our quarterback), as he was not performing as well as he had led us to believe he could. He tended to have a rather negative attitude towards the game, and was reluctant to turn up for training. As he had signed a contract we were obliged to honour the payment agreed; we also got him to sign a waiver to stop any adverse publicity, either here or in the United States.

Once again it was time to meet the Storm-Bombadiers in the return match, which we needed to win. In view of the events of the previous week, we asked Allan Brown to take the job of quarterback, to which he agreed. The opening was a miscellany of errors, and it wasn't until Conroy Brown recovered a fumble, that Steve Donegal was able to open the scoring after a five-yard rush, with no extra point: 6–0. In the second quarter, the Storm were backed up on their own ten-yard line. The snap was too high and the ball sailed out of the end zone for a two-point safety: 8–0. On their next drive, the Pioneers drove downfield to the thirteen-yard line, from where Steve Donegal powered in and added the extra point himself: 15–0. The Pioneers continued to dominate, with Allan Brown connecting with Clive Etienne for a nineteen-yard reception plus the extra point from Steve Donegal: 22–0.

The Pioneers momentarily lost concentration in the third quarter to allow the Storm to score, bringing it to 22–6. There were no further points added during the rest of the period, or incidentally the rest of the game.

The win should see the Pioneers in the semi-final, a very commendable result for their first season in Division 1.

We now had to face the league leaders, Birmingham Bulls, in back-to-back matches. The first was at home in Fenny Stratford, and the Pioneers were determined to show that they were ready and willing to take on all comers.

At the start, Ryan Holness recovered a fumble to set up a field goal attempt, which was unsuccessful. On the next play, Ryan Holness intercepted a pass, but the Pioneers were unable to capitalise on it. The Bulls opened the scoring following an interception with a touchdown and point after: 0–7. The Pioneers retaliated with a completed twenty-nine-yard catch from Ryan Holness to Steve Sobers for the touchdown but no point after: 6–

7. After numerous errors from the Pioneers, the Bulls added a further twenty unanswered points to make the half-time score 6–27.

The second half began with the Bulls scoring on their first three drives including one two-point and one one-point conversion to bring the score to 6–48. The Pioneers finished the game with a bit of razzle-dazzle following a Graham Scrace interception return of thirty-two yards for Ryan Holness to complete a pass to Steve Sobers for his second touchdown making the final score 12–48. It must be noted that Ryan Holness was unique in completing all his passes from the running back position, which is unusual at any level of the game.

We arrived in Solihull with a squad of only twenty-five players for the return match against the Bulls, and once again it was the defense that prevented a complete whitewash. The Bulls opened the scoring at the start of the first quarter with six points, and then they did it again just before the end putting them thirteen points up: 0–13. In the second period, the Bulls added two more scores, adding the point after to the first, but missing the second: 0–26. The Pioneers got on the scoreboard through a mistake by the Bulls. They were held close to their own end zone and were forced to punt. The snap was too high and went out of the zone for a two-point safety: 2–26.

The Pioneers fought gallantly in the third quarter and succeeded to limit the Bulls to just one touchdown: 2–32. The final score came in the last period, with the Bulls completing a fifteen-yard pass plus the extra point: 2–39.

Not one of our best performances, but a gutsy show nonetheless.

For the final game of the regular season we travelled to London to face the Olympians, who had beaten us soundly at the last meeting. The Pioneers' first drive faltered and London took over on downs; they then proceeded to drive downfield to score with a six-yard reception and added the point after: 0–7. There was no further score as the Pioneers' defense held firm. The second quarter was again a battle, with the Pioneers being unable to capitalise on some promising plays. However, the Olympians showed their superiority and managed to add a further seven points to make it 0–14 at the half.

Following the break, the fired up Pioneers denied London any further score until late in the final period, when the Olympians completed a drive with a two-yard rush, but were denied the extra point. Final score: 0–20.

The scoreline wasn't very pretty, but nevertheless the two teams were in contention in the semi-final to be played at Southwark Park in London.

I don't believe I mentioned it before, but during this season we had an American come down to some games in an advisory role. His name was Mike Sidney, and he's based at RAF Lakenheath. We hoped to possibly persuade him to become involved with the coaching in future.

The semi-final was played in 85–90° heat with a depleted squad due to injuries, and we also fielded a replacement quarterback, Simon Sparkes, who had last played for us some three years ago. In spite of these drawbacks, the Pioneers drew first blood, following an interception by Ryan Holness, with the ball being returned forty-nine yards to set up a five-yard rush by Clive Ellington for the score: 6–0.

The second quarter was a catalogue of penalties and turnovers, resulting in London scoring three unanswered touchdowns plus a two-point conversion: 6–20.

After the break, and in spite of further injuries, the Pioneers held London to a scoreless third quarter. But inevitably the Olympians managed to add a further six points in the last period, making the final score 6–26.

It was quite an achievement by the Pioneers to attain the semi-final in their first season in Division 1, and we could look forward to even greater success in the following year.

The annual Dinner Dance was again a great success and it was held at the Friendly Lodge in Two Mile Ash. Our guests of honour were the Secretary of the Hockey Association and his wife, and it was this year that I was honoured to receive the Clubman of the Year award.

As I mentioned earlier, the league had tried to ban Tyrone Lindsey for life. I also mentioned that Tyrone Lindsey had taken a year off. When I contacted the league they were still very vague, and I requested copies of all the evidence. As this was not forthcoming I approached a solicitor to take the case for us. Despite writing several letters, the situation was no nearer a solution. Finally we contacted the league again, and said that as no move had been taken to verify the matter, we would assume that time had run out and we would carry on and sign Tyrone Lindsey. We heard no more.

## 1996

This year, John Parker and Allan Brown decided to stand down as coaches, so we signed Mike Sidney as Head Coach. As I said, Mike had been with us at some of the previous season's games, so he was no stranger to the team. Mike was based with the US Air Force at Lakenheath, as I said earlier, and travelled whenever he could to training, depending on his service commitments. As stated earlier, we signed Tyrone Lindsey as well in the position of Defensive Coach. While on the subject of new signings I'd like to put on record two players of note. First there was Pete Underwood, who was quarterback in 1994 for the Bedford Bombadiers, who if you remember we beat in the final to gain promotion. (He also played for us back in 1993.) Secondly there was Dennis Soraghan, a player from the Irish International Team, and he travelled every weekend from his home in Dublin to play or train. A truly dedicated and inspirational player, he was a big asset to the team.

As observed earlier, the committee had reduced, with people finding they couldn't continue so it finally came down to just Margaret, Brian Day, Dave Lane and myself to manage the club. The team had also seen a lot of top class players wanting to join us, which boosted our egos significantly and gave us the potential to put the Pioneers at the top.

This season we were to christen our new venue, the National Hockey Stadium. The facilities were the best we had encountered, even though they were a bit expensive, but 'you gets what you pays for', as they say. The visiting teams and officials wholeheartedly agreed.

The one drawback we found was that the pitch was enclosed with a metal fence, which could be a hazard. So I contacted the London Monarchs, the England professional team, and asked if I could borrow the padding that they used for their games. Imagine my surprise when they agreed and sent ninety-two pads in an articulated lorry! Unfortunately, when it arrived there was only the driver and myself there to unload. All we could do was to stack the pads inside the outer wall of the stadium until I could organise somewhere to store them.

I was at the stadium early the following morning, and together with a couple of lads who worked at the stadium we managed to get them under cover below the stand. The other problem we had concerned the goalposts. I discovered that to put them in position we would need a JCB. This was because there were nets at each end of pitch, to contain any balls that would otherwise have gone astray. Our goalposts, because of the swan neck design, had the main post outside the fence, and the crossbar inside, hence the need to assemble them first, then lift them over the nets. The first time we tried it was a bit of a nightmare, but with time we became quite adept.

When it came to marking out the pitch, the Hockey Association insisted that the lines must be easily washed off. This meant that I had to do some research to find the right material. I finally found a firm based in Hinckley, and consulted them about the problem. After travelling to their factory twice, I found out that they supplied our local council with this material, and that the stadium already employed them for marking out the pitch for other sports. Although I was a little bit miffed at not being told this at the beginning, still it solved the problem.

Once again the schedule for the season looked quite formidable, with teams like Basildon Chiefs, Sussex Raiders, Plymouth Admirals, Sheffield Cyclones and Brighton Laker B52s, including two inter-conference games against Redbridge Fire and Leicester Panthers.

As the stadium would not be available early in the season due to previous bookings, it was just as well that our first games were away, beginning with the Basildon Chiefs.

We had signed a new American quarterback by the name of Mike Wilson. I drove up to Heathrow with Dave Lane to meet him. His flight arrived but there was no sign of him. On making enquiries, we found out that there seemed to be a problem with his work permit, and he was being detained in the immigration office. Dave and I finally managed to persuade the authorities that everything was above board and we made our way down to the car park. When we arrived I couldn't find the car and reported to an attendant that it had been stolen. Imagine my embarrassment when he came back and pointed out that I was on the wrong floor!

Our first game was away to the Basildon Chiefs, who won the coin toss and elected to receive. On their first drive the Pioneers held them to no gain. The Pioneers took over the ball on the Chiefs' thirty-seven-yard line, and on the first play, Nigel Fleming rushed for twelve yards; there was no gain on the next play but on the third play Pete Underwood completed a twenty-five-yard pass to Steve Sobers for the touchdown and another pass for the two points: 8–0. The Chiefs' continued inability to move the ball allowed the Pioneers to add a further eight points, with a rushing touchdown from Nigel Fleming before the change of ends: 16–0. The Chiefs rallied in the second quarter, but with some excellent defensive play the Pioneers denied them any score.

Following the break the Chiefs rallied and managed to get the ball into the end zone, only to have it called back for offensive pass interference. It was in the third quarter that we put our new quarterback on the field. As I said earlier, his name was Mike Wilson and he had only been in the country for two days. His debut seemed very promising; however, this proved to be the only game he would take part in, as I will explain later.

There was no further score until late in the last period. With about eight minutes left in the game, Pete Underwood (who was back on the pitch) threw a twenty-four-yard pass to Steve Sobers, who was knocked out of bounds on the one-yard line. On the next play, Nigel Fleming rushed the necessary yardage for the third touchdown, followed by a successful two-point conversion. Final score: 24–0.

As I said, Mike Wilson only played for a very short time, and when I called round to take him to training the following week, the player he was staying with told me that he had disappeared. It transpired that he had gone back to the States because he said he was homesick. This made me very angry, as we had paid his return fare, and he had signed a contract. We were going to sue him, but on taking legal advice decided to leave well alone and learn by our experience.

We travelled to Crawley for our next game against the Sussex Raiders. We were plagued by gale force winds and rain, and the team struggled to find their form. Sussex did very well in the first quarter. With a severe crosswind making passing difficult, they managed to complete a pass into the end zone to open the scoring with no extra point: 0–6.

It wasn't until the second period that the Pioneers began to show their form, with some fine running from Nigel Fleming, and their determination paid finally off with a three-yard pass to Clive Etienne to even the scores at 6–6.

After the break, the Pioneers kept up the pressure and following an impressive drive managed a second touchdown with a nine-yard pass to Clive Etienne. Steve Donegal rushed for the two points: 14–6.

The final period was marred by penalties and some dubious decisions by the officials, which nearly cost the Pioneers the game. In the dying seconds the Raiders, through a penalty, were on their own two-yard line. They rushed through to score their second touchdown, but the attempted conversion was thwarted, allowing the Pioneers to claim the win: 14–12.

The following Sunday we travelled to Redbridge in North London to play the first of our inter-conference games. Our opponents were the Redbridge Fire, and we were determined to show them just what we could do.

There was no sign of what was to come as the Pioneers slipped behind through sloppy play, allowing the Fire to capitalise on an interception to open the scoring: 0–6. They – the Pioneers – finally turned the game round with a flourish towards the end of the first quarter. The first score came from a six-yard pass to Paul Skelly with the two points added by Nigel Fleming for 8–6. The second was from a superb run of seventy-six yards by Steve Donegal, and Steve Sobers added the two points: 16–6. The Pioneers hit overdrive in the second quarter by adding three unanswered touchdowns, one from a thirty-yard catch by Joe Greenidge, no point after, one from a one-yard run by Clive Ellington, again no point after, and finally a seven-yard run from Stuart Brereton plus two points by Clive Etienne: 36–6.

After the break, the Pioneers continued to apply pressure and added two further scores from Clive Etienne with the first an eight-yard catch, no point after, and a nine-yard catch plus two points from Joe Greenidge: 50–6. In the final period, the Pioneers made one more score from a two-yard catch by Paul Skelly, with no point after. A second touchdown was called back through a penalty. Final score: 56–6, altogether a resounding victory.

Now it was our turn to make the journey to Plymouth; after all, they'd had to do the journey twice to us. I hired a coach for two days, as we travelled down on the Saturday. It was very disappointing, as after I'd paid a lot of money to hire the coach, a lot of the players went in their own vehicles, leaving me with about a dozen on board. The lads who travelled on the coach with Margaret, Brian and I stayed at a youth hostel, which turned out to be very basic, but very reasonable. Dennis Soraghan, our player from Ireland, flew into Plymouth Airport on the Sunday morning, and it wasn't until after the game that we found out that there was no flight out of Plymouth, so we had to give Dennis a lift back to Gatwick.

We had met Plymouth several times before, but this was the first time on their home ground, and I must say they made us very welcome.

The Pioneers won the toss and decided to put Plymouth's offense on first. The first quarter resulted in both teams being unable to make the end zone, as they sized each other up. At the start of the second quarter the teams began to show more determination, and the Admirals opened the scoring with a ten-yard pass but failed to add the extra point: 0–6. This roused the Pioneers, who shortly afterwards equalised with a six-yard reception by Steve Sobers, evening the scores at 6–6.

After the break, the Pioneers began to dominate the game with good defense. It was the offense that increased the score with a ten-yard rush by Nigel Fleming to raise the score to 12–6. In the final quarter, on a bungled play, the Pioneers put a further two points on the board with a safety from Tom Cregg: 14–6. Then, to round off the scoring, the quarterback, Pete Underwood, succeeded with a twenty-eight-yard rush on a quarterback keep, with Clive Etienne adding the two points to make the final score 22–6.

A defensive player who rates a mention here is our American friend, Jose Surita, who had been an inspiration to our defense since he joined the club.

Our next match was our first home game of the season, and our opponents were the Sussex Raiders. Because of unforeseen difficulties we were unable to use the Hockey Stadium, so we had to search around to find another venue. We were very lucky because one of our players worked for the Americans at the Upper Heyford Air Force Base and managed to arrange for us to play at RAF Croughton, which was a satellite base, where, if you remember, we had played before. They offered us the use of the camp playing field and also the changing facilities, for which we were very grateful. Also we had an audience of the families of the men stationed on the camp, and they were very surprised at how well we had learnt to play their national game.

The Raiders kicked off but were unable to move the ball. Then the Pioneers took over and on their first possession Clive Ellington scored with a twenty-four-yard rush and Ken Barnett added the two points: 8–0. This was quickly followed by Ken Barnett breaking tackles and rushing thirty-five yards to score, no point after: 14–0. Before the end of the quarter Clive Ellington added a further six points with a seven-yard sprint. No point after: 20–0. The second quarter was again dominated by the Pioneers' defense.

Our next opponents were our old adversaries, Brighton Laker B52s (a new name). This was the first game to be played at the Hockey Stadium, and everybody was impressed with the facilities we had to offer, for the teams, the officials and the spectators.

The Pioneers began the game with a flourish, with Nigel Fleming scoring the first touchdown with a nine-yard rush: 6–0. In the second quarter, the Pioneers began to show their determination, with Paul Skelly scoring the second touchdown after a forty-seven-yard reception: 12–0. Then Clive Etienne completed a six-yard catch to make it 18–0 at the half.

The Pioneers maintained the pressure after the break, with Clive Etienne completing a fourteen-yard reception plus the two-point conversion from Pete Underwood: 26–0. Ken Barnett was the next player to score, but no point after: 32–0. Then our Irish player, Dennis Soraghan, completed the scoring to make the final score 38–0. The Pioneers once again showed just how much their technique had improved over the season, making them a force to be reckoned with.

The way the season was going, if we could keep up the momentum, we were in with the chance of winning the championship and a chance to play in Europe.

Our next visitors to the stadium were the Basildon Chiefs for the return match, which we hoped to win to keep us on course for the championship.

Both teams stalled on their first possessions, then, following another Chiefs' punt, the Pioneers put in a double reverse play which completely foxed both the defense and some of our own offense, and allowed Pete Underwood the quarterback to scamper thirty-six yards for the opening score, Dennis Soraghan added the two points to make it 8–0.

Early in the second quarter the Chiefs rallied, scored a touchdown from a thirty-yard catch and added the extra point: 8–7. The Pioneers hit back and scored three touchdowns from Clive Ellington (one) and Steve Sobers (two) with Clive Etienne and Ken Barnett each adding two points bringing the score at halftime to 30–7.

After the break, the Pioneers continued to dominate, and Clive Etienne scored two more touchdowns but no points after: 42–7. Clive Ellington then added the next touchdown, plus the two points, to raise the score to 50–7. In the final period, it was Clive Etienne who scored the last touchdown, to give a resounding result of 56–7.

This result clinched the Conference title for the Pioneers; it was then that we learnt that Brighton had withdrawn from the league, so were unable to play the return match, so we were awarded the win, 1–0, by default. This made the team 8–0 on the season with two games to play, and a guaranteed place in the semi-final.

It was now our turn to welcome our old friends Plymouth Admirals to our new premises for the season's penultimate match. After being shown around, they were very impressed with the way everything was laid out, and once again their fans were very voluble. It was Ken Barnett who put the first points on the board with a six-yard run, plus the point after 6–0, and although Plymouth squared the match 6–6, the Pioneers got down to some serious football in the second quarter, scoring thirty-five unanswered points with touchdowns from Gladstone McKenzie, Ken Barnett (two) And Stuart Brereton, with two-point conversions from Ken Barnett, Steve Sobers and Steve Donegal: 41–6.

After the break, Ken Barnett scored another touchdown, with Roland Quaye adding the two points. Gladstone McKenzie got his second touchdown from ten yards in the fourth quarter with Roland Quaye again collecting the two points. Then with twenty-four seconds left in the game, Steve Sobers scored with a twelve-yard catch and Stuart Brereton gained the two points. As usual the score does not reflect the intensity of the game, and Plymouth were magnanimous in defeat, and wished us well in the semi-final.

The final game of the regular season was an inter-conference match against the Leicester Panthers, who in the past had defeated us every time we met. With a record season so far behind us, we were determined to reverse this situation.

I was supposed to be on holiday at this time, but I couldn't bear to miss this very important game. So I sent Margaret off on the Saturday and I travelled up by train on the Sunday night. By the way, our destination was Inverness, and the result of the match made it all worthwhile, as you will see.

The game was played before a very noisy crowd and was one of the best attendances we had enjoyed for a very long time. The first quarter was scoreless as both teams sized each other up. Then Steve Sobers put the Pioneers in the lead with a touchdown but no point after: 6–0. The Panthers replied with a field goal to trail at 6–3. The Pioneers then drove the length of the field for Ken Barnett to score and leave the Pioneers 12–3 at the half.

After the break, Gary Gonsalves made a thirty-seven-yard interception return for a touchdown: 18–3. Clive Etienne added another touchdown to stretch the lead to 24–3 going into the final quarter. Paul Skelly added the Pioneers' next touchdown, before the Panthers hit back with two scores of their own: 30–15. Dean McBroom scored the Pioneers' final touchdown, and incidentally gained 329 yards on offense on the day. Final score: 36–15.

We were very pleased at having finally vindicated ourselves and shown all and sundry that the Pioneers were definitely on a roll. We had now reached the semi-final with an unbeaten record of 10–0, and now we wanted to go on and reach the final.

On the day of the semi-final, I was at the stadium at 8 a.m. To supervise the marking of the pitch and the erection of a bouncy castle we had hired for the kiddies. Of course, I was not on my own, as several people, who were regular helpers, arrived to give a hand. The flags had to be hoisted, the Union Jack, the Stars and Stripes and the club flag (which I made myself from a sheet I scrounged off of Margaret, as mentioned before). The pitch had to be checked and cleared of any bits of rubbish that might prove a hazard to players; because of the nature of the game, they spent a fair amount of time lying down. At last all the preparations were complete, the teams were present and were performing their callisthenics prior to the kick-off.

I forgot to mention that our opposition came from the Sheffield Cyclones, who were a team newly formed this year, but consisted of a number of very experienced players and were not going to be a walkover.

The first quarter saw the Pioneers open the scoring with a twelve-yard rush from Steve Sobers, with no point after: 6–0. Sheffield, not to be outdone, replied with a similar score, making it 6–6 at the change of ends. In the second quarter, the Cyclones raised their score by six points with a brilliant thirty-two-yard run but no point after: 6–12. It was now the Pioneers' turn to engineer a drive, which Gladstone McKenzie finished off with a two-yard rush, followed by Steve Sobers adding the two extra points. So at the half the score was 14–12.

After the break, Clive Etienne made the end zone with a twenty-yard catch, but the two-point attempt was intercepted and run back for two points, putting the score at 20–14. The Pioneers then stepped up the pressure and added a brace of touchdowns, one from Gladstone McKenzie plus two points from Ken Barnett; the other touchdown was from Steve Donegal on a one-yard rush but no point after: 34–14.

Then, with five minutes left in the game, we had to suspend it for fifteen minutes due to lightning and torrential rain. When the teams returned, Sheffield snatched a final touchdown to add six more points, making the final score 34–20. Despite being a new team, as mentioned earlier, the Cyclones put on a superb performance, and would be a team to be reckoned with in 1997.

We now had to prepare for the Division 1 Bowl to be played at the stadium in Saffron Lane, Leicester. This decision was despite the league coming down to inspect the Hockey Stadium with a view to holding the final there. The official who turned up was given a conducted tour of the facilities by the stadium manager and myself and was full of praise, and remarked that it was much better than Leicester. The excuse given for not using the stadium was that it was too expensive.

When we arrived at the stadium we were told that we couldn't use the changing rooms due to an infestation of rats, so we were sent half a mile up the road to a Leisure Centre, where we had to contend with an Indian wedding party. It was a very unsatisfactory arrangement and we lodged a complaint with the league.

The game was dominated by defense and penalties, resulting in the Pioneers losing very narrowly in their bid for the championship in only their second season in Division 1. It was devastating after posting a perfect season's unbeaten record. It was the Pioneers who scored first when Ryan Holness intercepted a pass, which he returned fifty-nine yards with no extra point: 6–0. There was no further score before they changed ends, but at the start of the second quarter the Panthers drove down to the Pioneers' one-yard line, from there they evened the score and kicked the extra point to lead 6–7. Then later in the period the Panthers got downfield in a position to kick a field goal, making the score 6–10.

The second half developed into a defensive battle with neither side giving any quarter, thus ensuring that the scoreline remained unchanged.

Unfortunately for us, Mike Sidney was posted back to the States, so once again the position of Head Coach was vacant. After some deliberation we decided to promote Tyrone Lindsey to the post, as he had been with us through the season as Defensive Coordinator and had proved he was capable.

Also, by now the committee had dwindled down to just five, myself as general manager, Brian Day as Secretary, Margaret as Treasurer, Tom Cregg as P/R manager and Derek Dodds as Equipment Manager; we had no Team Manager as we were waiting for someone to be elected.

Now that the season was finished, we entered into talks with the other top teams with a view to break away from the Senior League and form a new league, a sort of Champions League composed of six teams. The teams involved were: Milton Keynes Pioneers, Sheffield Cyclones, London Olympians, Birmingham Bulls, Leicester Panthers and Manchester Force, to be known as the 'Big Six'. We had several meetings to establish how we would introduce the concept, and it was at one of these meetings that I was introduced to John Carney. He was with Tyrone Lindsey and he was telling us of his plans to boost the image of British American Football, which were a little bit over the top, as you will find out. Also at one of our meetings, the delegates from Manchester Force attended to present their portfolio, as they were a newly formed team and we had to vet them to see if they had the necessary expertise to compete at our level. The portfolio was accepted and we continued with our plans.

However, it was not to be, as news came through that Leicester had folded, and Manchester were non-starters. The remaining four teams sat down to some serious discussions about the implications, and it was decided that, as we had come this far, we would continue with the formation of the league with a revised title of the 'Big C'. The Senior League were a bit upset by our decision and intimated that it would be difficult for us to rejoin the Senior League if things went awry. We applied to BAFA for recognition, and eventually it was agreed that we had their backing. With Leicester folding it meant that Milton Keynes were now recognised as the National Champions, which in turn meant that we had the opportunity to represent England in Europe. There followed protracted negotiations with the European League, and we discovered that we would need a lot of money, as initially we would have to post a £4,000 bond. In addition, we would be required to pay our travelling expenses, except for a stipulated amount from the home team.

The Dinner Dance for this year we held at the Shenley Church Inn, and this time we experimented with a running buffet. I must admit it was not an unqualified success, as any latecomers found that the food had run out. However, it was still a good night out, and as it turned out it was the last time that we would hold such an event. The recipient of the Clubman of the Year award this time was Tyrone Lindsey for his efforts as Defensive Coach.

# *1997*

This year we managed to negotiate a sponsorship deal with our local radio station, 103FM Horizon Radio, we agreed to incorporate their name with ours making us the Horizon Pioneers. As regards sponsorship, I had always said that under no circumstances would I change the name of the club to suit a sponsor. If it came to a vote within the committee and it was agreed to change the name, then I would resign. I recall two instances of teams doing just that and one of them regretting it. The team was the Cambridge County Cats and they won a sponsorship deal with an apple company on the condition that they changed their name to Cambridge Crunchers. All went well until the end of the season when the sponsor pulled out and they reverted back to their title, but to my mind they had lost a lot of their integrity. The other team was Bedford, who were initially known as the Bedford Stags. The Charles Wells Brewery sponsored them provided that they changed their name to the Bombadiers after one of the brewer's beers. Still, they did retain the name and the sponsor for some years. We also had a local car dealer as a sponsor, Bletchley Motor Group. These were not sponsorships for money. The radio company gave us daily coverage on air, announcing games and any other relevant information, and BMG arranged, and paid for, the printing of posters and tickets.

The team also featured on Jim Davidson's *Generation Game*, which I felt was a bit of a flop, as not enough planning went into what was done on the night. I was not involved in the planning or execution of the event, as all the preparation was conducted in London. Still, it got us a mention on television nationwide.

Having only four teams in the 'Big C' meant that we would only be playing six regular season games, plus a semi-final and final. This short season meant that we would have several rest weeks, which was not good for team morale, but at least we had an extra game to be played in Europe. We were informed that our opposition in Europe would be the Paris Mousquetaires, and the game was scheduled to take place in Paris to be played on 17 May 1997, a win would see us in the European semi-final against Austria or Italy.

*Pioneers, 1997*
*This is the team as it was that year*

Firstly we will deal with the first of the regular season's games, where we were drawn against the Birmingham Bulls. If you remember we had played them in 1995, and we were soundly beaten both times, so now it was time for retribution.

The first quarter was a scrappy affair, littered with penalties, and it was the Bulls who capitalised on the chaos with a field goal, to open the scoring at 0–3. The rest of the quarter remained scoreless as both defenses blocked every attempt to add points. The Bulls added a further three points with a second field goal in the next period to make it 0–6 before the Pioneers finally got their act together. The Pioneers thought they had levelled the score through Ken Barnett, but his knee had touched the ground on the one-yard line. However, three plays later, following a five-yard penalty, they made the touchdown when Pete Underwood connected on a six-yard pass to Jeremy Simms to even the score at half-time: 6–6.

It was a fired up Pioneers who came out for the second half. The offense now started to dominate when Alan Tait, an ex-London Monarch, scored his first touchdown for the club by pulling in a sixteen-yard pass to make the score 12–6. The defense then got in on the act when Albert Case sacked the quarterback in the end zone for a two-point safety, after chasing him for twenty yards: 14–6. In the fourth quarter, the running game came to the forefront with Stuart Brereton and Clive Ellington ripping the Bulls' defense apart. It was Clive Ellington who made the play of the game by breaking through for a thirty-seven-yard touchdown, with Alan Tait adding the extra point to bring the final score to 21–6. Altogether a rewarding result to boost our confidence.

It was now time for us to make our debut in the European arena with the game against the Paris Mousquetaires. To say it was a disaster is understating the situation, as I will now explain.

It all began in London. Some of us met the coach at the Scratchwood services, where we arranged to park our cars overnight. We then went on to Marble Arch, where we had arranged for the players to meet the coach at midday. This, we reckoned, should give us plenty of time to catch the 3 p.m. ferry from Dover. All went well until one of the players – no names, no pack drill, as they say – turned up in his car and refused to pay the parking charge; so, against our better judgement, we chased him all over London until he finally parked in a street. We then made our way to Dover, as quickly as possible, to catch the ferry, only to find that, because of the delay, we had missed the boat by five minutes. We then had to wait until 6 p.m. for the next available ship.

Arriving in Calais at around 7.30 p.m. we started out for Paris and about halfway there we had to stop for a drink and a snack. Resuming our journey, we finally arrived in Paris and started looking for our hotel. Unfortunately there were several hotels with the same name, and it wasn't until almost 2 a.m. that we found the right one; it was then that the drivers told us that they only had ten minutes left on their tachographs. By the time we got all the lads settled it was 3.30 a.m. and they had to be up again at 8 a.m. for a continental breakfast, which is neither fit for man nor beast, so they went off in search of something more substantial. So when we arrived at the ground to play, in rather hot and humid conditions, the lads were not only tired and hungry, but also rather grumpy, to say the least. We also had language problems, as we found it virtually impossible to convey to the staff there our need for water on the sidelines.

The Pioneers received the ball and drove downfield, only to be thwarted by an interception close to the end zone. Paris took over the ball but the Pioneers' defense denied them the opportunity to score, ensuring the first quarter remained scoreless.

The second quarter was set in the same mould until Paris managed to break through and score, plus adding the two points: 0–8. There was no further score before the end of the half.

Following the break the Pioneers appeared to have settled down, but with penalties and some critical mistakes they allowed Paris to increase their lead by a further eight points making it 0–16.

It seemed the Pioneers would achieve some success in the final period, but it was not to be. With about five minutes to go to the final whistle, the Mousquetaires scored once more, but were denied the extra point: 0–22.

It must be said that the Pioneers put on a sterling performance in difficult conditions, not all due to the weather. So ended our first foray into international sport, but it was worth the experience.

Incidentally, the player who was responsible for the unfortunate series of events at the outset of this adventure got quite a surprise when we dropped him off to collect his car. It transpired that the police, in their wisdom, had towed his car away, and he had to collect it from the pound, which I understand cost him £130. Now, if he had parked it at Marble Arch it would have cost about £30. So I have a feeling that he wished he had listened to us in the first place and parked where we told him. Still, he lived to regret his rash action.

The second conference game for the Pioneers was against Sheffield Cyclones. This game should have been played away, but Sheffield were unable to guarantee a venue, and as the Hockey Stadium was also unavailable, we approached Manor Fields to see if they would allow us to play the game there. They agreed when we told them that the game was to be played in aid of Great Ormond Street Children's Hospital.

In extremely windy conditions, the Pioneers kicked off, and Sheffield's first drive foundered and they were forced to punt. The Pioneers first possession saw Clive Ellington gain twenty-one rushing yards, which bode well, as a few plays later Steve Donegal took the ball in from seventeen yards and added two extra points to open the scoring at 8–0. The remainder of the quarter saw both defenses hold firm to deny any further score.

In the second quarter, the Pioneers added a further six points with an eight-yard reception by Jeremy Simms but no extra point: 14–0. In the ensuing plays the Pioneers seemed to lose touch momentarily, which allowed the Cyclones to score twice with no extra points, bringing the half-time score to 14–12.

Following the break the Pioneers stepped up a gear, with Clive Ellington adding another six points with no extras: 20–12. Again the teams denied each other any attempt to add to their scores, and it wasn't until well into the final period that the Pioneers managed to add a further eight points, with Ken Barnett making the touchdown and Dennis Soraghan adding the extra two points to make the final score 28–12.

It was an historic day for the Horizon Pioneers, playing before a crowd of 2,000 plus in the prestigious National Hockey Stadium, against the Birmingham Bulls. If you remember we won the away match back in May, and we were geared up to do it again.

From the kick-off the Pioneers took the match by the scruff of the neck and proved that they were a team to be reckoned with. The Horizon Pioneers kicked off and the Bulls' opening drive was short lived. On the Pioneers' first possession, Pete Underwood engineered a drive to the Bulls' one-yard line, from where he sneaked over for the score, though the attempt for the point after was no good: 6–0. The rest of the quarter was a defensive battle with neither team gaining the upper hand. This situation was repeated in the second quarter, which remained scoreless: 6–0.

After the break, the Pioneers showed their dominance by adding three unanswered scores with firstly an eleven-yard catch by Roland Quaye. The second was a superb one-handed catch by Mo Washington and the third was the result of a twenty-seven-yard rush by Stuart Brereton, who appeared to have been stopped four times, none of the point after attempts were successful, making the score at this point 24–0.

The final quarter was again dominated by both defenses until Joshua West pulled in a dazzling one-handed catch of forty-nine yards and scampered into the end zone to increase the final tally to 30–0. Altogether a very memorable day, and hopefully a step forward in increasing public support for the sport.

Also after the final whistle our sponsor, 103FM Horizon Radio, presented a trophy for the best offensive player to Steve Donegal, and for the best defensive player Albert Case.

The Horizon Pioneers suffered their first defeat of the season (excluding the French game) playing the London Olympians in atrocious weather conditions in South London. They had to cope not only with torrential rain, but also lightning, which suspended the game twice. The 'O's kicked off and the Pioneers' first drive faltered and they were forced to punt, and although the snap was high the kicker managed to loft the ball thirty yards. On their following drive the Pioneers were forced back, by penalties, to their ten-yard line, the ensuing snap was too high and went over the kicker's head and out of the end zone for a two-point safety: 0–2. Three plays later, three players were ejected from the game for infringement of the rules, one from the Pioneers and two from the 'O's. This meant that they would not be allowed to play in the next game. The second quarter was an energetic battle between both defenses denying any attempt to alter the scoreline. Half-time score: 0–2.

Following the break, the 'O's drove downfield, with the Pioneers giving up yardage with five penalties in a row, and London capitalised with a two-yard run for six points. The two-point conversion was attempted twice, because of yet another penalty, and the second time the 'O's crossed the line to make the score 0–10. It was during this period that the game had to be stopped for about five minutes because of lightning.

The fourth quarter was again stopped for a further fifteen minutes, again because of lightning. When play resumed, it developed into a defensive battle which neither team could break down, leaving the score at 0–10.

Two weeks later we had the return match against London at the Hockey Stadium, this time in ideal weather conditions, and we were looking to avenge the defeat from when we last met.

The whole of the first half was scoreless as neither team was able to break the deadlock.

After the break, the third quarter was also scoreless, and it wasn't until the final period that any impression was made. Early in the period, the Pioneers went for a field goal, which was successful, but was nullified by a London penalty of roughing the kicker. This gave the Pioneers the opportunity for Nigel Fleming to power over the line for the points: 6–0. On the next drive, London had to punt from close to their own end zone. The snap was high and sailed over the head of the kicker. He tried to kick it out but missed and Stuart Brereton recovered it for a touchdown. This time Gavin Hart's kicked point after was good, raising the score to 13–0.

On their next possession, the Pioneers increased the pressure and Alan Tait caught a fifteen-yard pass with no point after to increase the score to 19–0. Finally in the dying seconds of the game, Stuart Brereton broke through the Olympian's defense to scamper forty-two yards to score, and Gavin Hart kicked for the point after, so the score rose to 26–0. A very gratifying result, as we had been beaten so many times before.

For the last game of the regular season, we travelled to Barnsley to take on the Sheffield Cyclones once again. This was a match, which if the Pioneers won, would put them at the top of the conference, and into the final.

The match began with both teams unable to make much headway and having to punt, until Alan Tait opened the scoring with a three-yard reception for the touchdown; the point after attempt failed: 6–0. Shortly afterwards Stuart Brereton completed an eleven-yard run to increase the score, and Gavin Hart once more added the extra point: 13–0. Then before the end of the quarter Alan Tait scored with a twenty-one-yard reception and Gavin Hart's extra point made it 20–0. The second period saw both defenses settle down to deny any further score before half-time.

After the break, the Horizon Pioneers changed quarterbacks, and with Steve Donlevy at the helm they drove downfield to set up a thirty-seven-yard field goal by Gavin Hart, giving us three more points for 23–0.

It wasn't until the fourth quarter that Sheffield rallied and scored on a twenty-two-yard reception to raise the score to 23–6. It was then that the Cyclones stunned everybody with an amazing ninety-yard reception for a touchdown, to which unfortunately they were unable to add the extra point: 23–12. However, the Pioneers were not finished yet as they once again scored, with Stuart Brereton adding a further six points with a fifteen-yard catch to make the final score 29–12.

This result put us in contention again with Sheffield in the semi-final, as they were second to Birmingham, who would be playing London 'O's in the other semi-final. Our match would have to be played elsewhere, as the Hockey Stadium was unavailable because of previous bookings. So I approached the company who had taken over the running of the National Bowl from the council, and asked if it would be possible for us to use the venue for the match. I mentioned that we had played at the Bowl before, which helped to sway the decision. We negotiated a deal which was agreed, with the proviso that we would have to supply mobile toilets for the spectators' convenience. We also brought in a small fair and a bouncy castle for the kiddies. I also had to arrange to sink new goalpost bases, as the ones that were already in the ground were of a completely different design. We dug the holes on the Friday and kept our fingers crossed that the cement would be dry in time for the game.

The game proved to be the toughest challenge of the season for the Pioneers, as they took on a vastly improved Sheffield team. Unfortunately the day was marred by the fact that we only had a crowd of about 700, which was a pity, as it turned out to be a nail-biting game.

From the kick-off both defenses stood firm, not allowing a score from either side. With a combination of good defense, and despite penalties, neither team was able to score, although they made the red zone several times, the situation remained the same throughout the whole of the first half.

After the break, the same strategy was repeated right throughout the third quarter, and it wasn't until late in the final period, and with only 3 minutes 27 seconds left in the game, that the Pioneers finally broke the deadlock with a nineteen-yard run by Mo Washington for the touchdown. The kick for the point after was successful: 7–0. Sheffield attempted to stage a comeback, but on the last play of the game they were intercepted.

This was the last match of one for our American players, Mo Washington, who left the country very shortly for service in Crete. He was sorely missed.

It was now time to gear up for the 'Big C' final to be played at the Hockey Stadium against the London 'O's. The game was played before the largest crowd of the year, indeed the largest crowd for many a year, numbering around 3,000. The weather too was hot and humid, making life a little unpleasant for the teams in their heavy kit.

On their first possessions, both teams failed to make any significant yardage and had to punt. On their second possession the Pioneers drove downfield to London's one-yard line from where Pete Underwood scored with a quarterback sneak, plus Gavin Hart kicked the extra point: 7–0. There were no further additions to the scoreboard during the rest of the period.

In the second quarter, London recovered and managed to score on two occasions, but could not add the extra points: 7–12. Despite further efforts, the score was destined to remain the same up to the half-time break.

After the break, in spite of heroic efforts, the third quarter was scoreless and it wasn't until the last period that things hotted up.

The Pioneers once again found themselves on London's one-yard line, from where Pete Underwood repeated the quarterback sneak for another touchdown and Gavin Hart making sure of the point after to make it 14–12. However, their lead was short-lived, as London replied with a fifty-three-yard catch and this time added the two extra points, raising the score to 14–20. Then in the closing seconds of the game Ken Barnett broke through from six yards to even the scores at 20–20. This bought up a nail-biting situation as the point after kick would mean an historic win for the Pioneers. However, it was not to be, as the kick was blocked, driving the game into sudden death overtime.

London won the toss to receive the ball first, and put a good drive together to reach the Pioneers' twelve-yard line, from where they scored the winning touchdown, making the final score 20–26.

It was during the match that John Carney kept on to me to go to the hospitality suite to meet some of his so-called potential sponsors. I told him that I had far too much to do on the sideline to worry about his daydreams. However, I did pop up just for a minute, and I must say I was not impressed as it appeared to me that mostly they were after the free booze etc., and in hindsight it seems that there was not a lot of sponsorship forthcoming. The game was recorded on television, but I have been unable to obtain a copy of the tape, over which I am very disappointed.

It was at this game, as it was the end of the season, that Margaret and I decided to retire: after all, we had managed the team successfully over eleven years and had taken them from being unknowns to National Champions. Of course, we had a lot of help along the way from a lot of very worthy people.

It was a very emotional time and Margaret was in tears. Then one of the players, Steve Sobers, grabbed a microphone and told the crowd who we were. The reaction from the spectators was very gratifying, and also the players gave us their support. Alas, we were completely ignored by the radio and television, as the two people we had nominated to take over hogged the media, boasting that they were the owners of the Pioneers. This claim was absolutely ludicrous, as they owned nothing but the name, and as you'll see they didn't own that for long.

The two people I referred to earlier were Tyrone Lindsey and a cohort of his, John Carney. As I have said, I was introduced to John Carney earlier in the season and I was not very impressed, as he seemed a bit of a wily character. The first thing they did was to form a limited company playing as the Pioneers. This was the start of the destruction of the Pioneers, as we had known them.

At the game we played at the National Bowl I had contacted the council to hire the play-bus and it was now that I received a telephone call from the council saying that the cheque I had paid them with had bounced. I was furious and telephoned Tyrone Lindsey and gave him a piece of my mind. I paid the amount myself and was finally reimbursed, after a lot of pushing.

After the final match, I was busy clearing up the stadium and Margaret was sitting in the dugout on the side of the pitch. The two men in question came out and engaged Margaret in conversation. Of course, I was too far away to hear what was said, but Margaret told me later that they had started moaning about how much money it was costing them. This was like a red rag to a bull, and Margaret blew her top and said in no uncertain terms, 'Don't you dare talk to me about money, you don't know the half of it.'

What she was referring to was the fact that over the years we had never claimed any money for expenses from the club; in fact, it was just the opposite, as all of the money came out of our own pockets, because if you remember I did mention Margaret taking out bank loans to support the club. This really took the wind out of their sails, and they just sat there dumbfounded and didn't dare mention it again.

With regard to the annual Dinner Dance, we were told that Tyrone Lindsey and John Carney were going to organise it. Their idea was to book a posh hotel in London and make it an evening dress occasion. This idea was thrown out by the team, as up to now all of our events had been very informal. Therefore, as I said earlier, that last year was the last of these functions, and we were all rather sad.

# *1998*

With the advent of the new year I personally felt at a loose end after the involvement of the last eleven years, and it was some time later that I found out that they (Lindsey and Carney) still owed the stadium £3,000 for last season, so the stadium management informed me that they were going to confiscate the goalposts and other equipment on Stadium premises in lieu of payment. It appears that the stadium was unable to trace John Carney or Tyrone Lindsey, so I assume that the debt is still outstanding.

The dream of the 'Big C' was very short-lived, as Sheffield folded, London and Birmingham returned to the Senior League, and the dubious duo had decided to take the Pioneers and attempt to get them into European Football. From reports I have had from various sources the scheme was a complete fiasco. They played one game in Paris and one game in Marseilles and had to do both the journeys by road, which, after our experience when we played in Paris, probably guaranteed that they would lose, which they did.

After this the team broke up and spread themselves around various other teams. Some went to the Olympians, Oxford Saints, Birmingham Bulls and London Mets; others went to Ipswich and Southern Sundevils. Margaret and I still try to attend games whenever possible as it's nice to be able to talk to the lads again, and 'Lady M' still gets her kiss and cuddle. Still, it's all very sad that after eleven years of hard work, and a lot of enjoyment, the team is now defunct. However, I still have all the trophies that the team won over the years, and we like to reflect on the good times we had and the wonderful people we met. I am at present trying to find somewhere where I can set up a trophy cabinet within the city, so that the achievements of the Pioneers are not completely lost. I recently contacted a local councillor (Mr Roger Bristow) to ask if there was any possibility of arranging somewhere in the

Civic Offices where I could locate a trophy cabinet. He mentioned the fact that there was a proposed stadium to be built in Bletchley, to accommodate the possible move of Wimbledon Football Club, and he suggested that I contact the man in charge, Mr Pete Winkleman, with a view to possibly locating the trophies in the new stadium. No result is at present available.

A very sad event occurred during this year and it took me completely by surprise. I had a visit from Christine Gaunt, a senior official from BAFA, with the news that Rudi Gumbs, of the Northants Storm, had died suddenly. Margaret had recently had an operation on her back, so I was very loath to leave her to attend the funeral. However, Christine had brought her daughter with her, and she volunteered to stay with Margaret so as I could go and pay my respects to an old friend.

Although I had retired, I was still in touch with the management of the England team, and I was contacted about a game they were planning against the French on 4 November, wanting to use the Hockey Stadium. I got in touch with the manager and arranged a meeting with the interested parties. All was arranged and I was asked if I would help out. Of course, I couldn't refuse, and they were very surprised when I told them that they would need to hire a JCB to install the gaol posts, they also asked me to arrange for a cherry picker for the video. I attended a couple of the training sessions and was very pleased to see several of the old Pioneers in the Great Britain side.

I was at the stadium at about 8 a.m. on the big day to help with the pitch marking, as the chap the stadium employed had never marked out an American Football field before. I also approached the council to borrow a French flag, as the only flags I had were the Stars and Stripes and the Union Jack, and on the day they were all flying. The game turned to be a well-fought battle, and the Lions came out the winners with a scoreline of 42–0 – a resounding victory, and sadly the last time I was actively involved.

## *2001*

As you can see by the absence of the last two years, I'd had no involvement with the sport except to attend a few games to support some of our old acquaintances. With regard to the equipment held at the stadium, I had a telephone call from the current manager of the stadium asking to see me. I made an appointment, as I was curious as to why he should want to see me. When we met it transpired that he wished to dispose of our goalposts and other odds and ends, so that they could utilise the space. I reminded him why the equipment was still on stadium premises, and he said that they had given up all hope of recovering the outstanding money. I said that I would do my best to find someone who might be interested, as I was still in contact with some of the existing teams. I also asked Brian Day if he would advertise the items on the Internet, but to no avail. I did manage to rescue the goalpost pads, which were quite expensive, and I have offered them to Brian Smallworth of the London Mets, as several of our old players have now registered with the team. I am still waiting to hear from him to make arrangements for their collection. As it happens, I eventually had to take the pads to Watford myself, and since then I have attended a few games, and I was very disappointed to see that they were not using them.

I don't think there is much more I can add, and I make no excuses for naming some of the players who helped enormously in the success of the Pioneers. Unfortunately, I cannot name all of the players, much as I would like to, as to be truthful I can't remember all of them. I did endeavour to make a list of all of the lads who played for us at one time or another and I was amazed than the number involved was in excess of 300!

Of course, there are many other people who gave freely of their time and assistance when it was needed. I'd like to take this opportunity to put my thanks on record to those that I have not already mentioned and some that I have. There was Andy Howe and his wife, Anita. Andy, besides working on the chain crew, was always on hand to help with the regular chores such as marking out the pitch, etc. I should mention Martin Grasby, who also helped with pitch marking, but also at the end of the games. He was one of the first to grab a sack and start collecting the rubbish and helping to store the equipment. Then there were my fellow committee members, Trina Collins, Gladstone McKenzie Sr, Dave Lane, who also kept the statistics of the games, and Brian Day. He was a great asset as a helper, and was also responsible for most of the contents of the programmes, of which we were very proud, as we provided a programme of at least twenty-eight pages, which were all articles, rules of the game, officials hand signals and, of course, the fixture list for the season. Advertising in the programmes was very hard to come by, as it appeared that people were not prepared to pay the reasonable fees that we stipulated. We did get some response, but I insisted that if necessary we would increase the number of pages rather than sacrifice our articles. Then there is Jeremy Hards, a dedicated supporter who travelled from Enfield to attend the games, and was also a member of the chain crew; Tony Reid, a man who became an essential addition to our work team, and gave unstintingly of his time; Kevin Dorrill, another supporter of a very generous nature, whose timely donations helped us achieve several of our aspirations; and Barry Nash, who coped extremely well as our first-aider.

The names go on and on, and it's great to know that because of these people the Pioneers became National Champions and represented their city and country.

Also one mustn't forget our group of dedicated cheerleaders who, with their chants and high spirits, helped the lads cope in times of disappointment. One girl in particular comes to mind; her name was Katy, and she joined the cheerleaders, the Buckeroos, way back in 1984, and remained with us right through to around 1994. If I remember rightly she finally left to get married.

## THE END

## *Afterthought*

I hope this attempt at trying to describe what it's like to be involved in sport has been educational and entertaining. I have tried to impart the feelings of achievement and also of disappointment that we felt during the years we were involved. Once again, I would like to convey my heartfelt thanks to everyone who was concerned with the Pioneers for their unstinting support through the highs and lows of the struggle for success. We can all hold our heads high and claim that we worked to uphold the club motto of 'Achievement through honesty and integrity', sometimes in the face of adversity. I make no apologies for the title I have chosen, as I honestly feel that despite representing Milton Keynes in Europe, even if only once, the team's name has been consigned to the archives.

Unfortunately, the sport in general appears to be in decline, as teams are either folding or merging through lack of support and the fact that there have been no concerted efforts to introduce youngsters into the sport. Of course, there are several youth teams around, but there are nowhere near enough youngsters to even try to supply the number of bodies needed to ensure the continued growth of the sport. The other thing is that for the junior teams the rules are being altered allegedly in the cause of safety, but I feel that they are taking away the essential part of the game – namely the contact side of the sport – and are making it too soft, thereby not preparing the lads for the undoubted ferocity of the senior game. Of course, there are kitted youth teams but I feel that they are introduced to this side of the sport too late for them to appreciate fully the impact it will have on them. During the years that I was involved, I was convinced that the administration of the league was lacking in initiative, as it seemed that the promotion of the sport was left to the teams. This situation did nothing to enhance the sport, and another big drawback was the fact that teams had to go 'cap in hand' to other organisations for permission to use their facilities, which was one reason that we played the summer season only.

# *Glossary: Guide to American Football Terms*

| | |
|---|---|
| *drive* | the movement of the offense downfield |
| *faked field goal* | an offense set-up for a goal attempt, but when the ball is snapped, it is either run or passed |
| *field goal* | a fourth down option, if yardage is considered achievable by a kick |
| *forced to punt* | a decision taken on fourth down, if required yardage is thought to be unattainable |
| *Hail Mary* | a very long pass attempt by the quarterback |
| *iron man game* | when players have to play both offense and defense |
| *PAT* | point after touchdown. Teams have the option to either run the ball or pass it. If run over the line they get one point; if PAT, two points |
| *quarterback keep* | the quarterback retains the ball when it's snapped and runs himself |
| *reception* | in which a wide receiver catches the ball |
| *red zone* | the area between the goal line and the twenty-yard line |
| *running back* | the player behind the quarterback who, when passed the ball, attempts to run through the defense |
| *sacked* | in which a defensive player gets through the line to tackle the quarterback before he can release the ball |
| *snap* | when the centre passes the ball to the quarterback |
| *turnover* | when the offense fumbles the ball or the defense intercepts it |

1938693R0010

Printed in Great Britain
by Amazon.co.uk, Ltd.,
Marston Gate.